ACCLAIM FOR *Lawrence Wright's*

REMEMBERING SATAN

"One of the real landmarks in journalism. The story itself is almost unutterably weird and would be fascinating no matter how well it was told but in the thoroughness of his reporting, and in his thoughtful treatment of the many issues the story touches, Wright has painted a perfect miniature of our time. . . . *Remembering Satan* is an edge-of-your-seat tale." —*Boston Globe*

"Skillfully and spellbindingly recounted."
—*San Francisco Chronicle*

"Brilliantly reported and compellingly written. . . . Wright persuasively challenges the entire 'recovered memory movement.'"
—*Texas Monthly*

"Wright is particularly good at giving a fair and succinct account of this troubling controversy." —*Chicago Tribune*

"[A] gripping and brilliantly constructed book."
—*The New York Review of Books*

"Wright makes brilliant use of this mind-boggling story to cast grave doubts on the whole notion of recovered-memory-syndrome. . . . Admirably, Wright delivers a cool-headed, meticulous account of the case." —*Entertainment Weekly*

"Compelling reading, expertly written. . . . Wright tells an incredible true story." —*Pittsburgh Post-Gazette*

"A cautionary tale about the dangers of so-called recovered memories. . . . *Remembering Satan* is stunning."
—*The New York Times Book Review*

Lawrence Wright
REMEMBERING
SATAN

Lawrence Wright is the author of *City Children, Country Summer; In the New World;* and *Saints and Sinners.* His articles have appeared in *Texas Monthly, Rolling Stone,* and *The New York Times Magazine.* He is a staff writer for *The New Yorker* and lives in Austin, Texas, with his wife and two children.

BOOKS BY LAWRENCE WRIGHT

Remembering Satan

Saints and Sinners

In the New World

City Children, Country Summer

REMEMBERING
SATAN

Lawrence Wright

———

REMEMBERING
SATAN

Vintage Books

A Division of Random House, Inc.

New York

FIRST VINTAGE BOOKS EDITION, MAY 1995

Copyright © 1994 by Lawrence Wright

All rights reserved under International and Pan-American
Copyright Conventions. Published in the United States by Vintage
Books, a division of Random House, Inc., New York, and
simultaneously in Canada by Random House of Canada Limited,
Toronto. Originally published in hardcover by
Alfred A. Knopf, Inc., New York, in 1994.

Portions of this work were originally published in *The New Yorker.*

The Library of Congress has catalogued the Knopf edition as
follows:
Wright, Lawrence.
Remembering Satan/ by Lawrence Wright. —1st ed.
p. cm.
ISBN 0-679-43155-1
1. False memory syndrome—United States—Case Studies. 2.
Ritual abuse victims—United States—Case studies. 3. Adult child
sexual abuse victims—United States—Case Studies. 4. Ingram,
Paul R.—Family. I. Title.
RC569.5.R59W75 1994
364.1'536—dc20 93-23561
CIP
Vintage ISBN: 0-679-75582-9

Author photograph © David MacKenzie

Manufactured in the United States of America
10 9 8 7

For Tina Brown

lucky star

Acknowledgments

This book first appeared, in large part, in *The New Yorker* magazine, and I am grateful for the wise counsel of my editor, Kim Heron, and the tireless assistance of fact checker Peter Wells. I also would like to thank the investigators in Olympia—Joe Vukich, Brian Schoening, Neil McClanahan, and Loreli Thompson—who were generous with their time and always helpful. Prosecutor Gary Tabor was always accommodating, and I thank him for his courtesy.

Elizabeth F. Loftus, at the University of Washington, has done much of the groundbreaking work on memory, and she afforded me a considerable amount of her valuable time and insight. Richard Ofshe, who has written about the Ingram case himself, was extremely helpful and insightful.

I owe a particular debt to Ethan Watters, a fine journalist who wrote about the Ingram case in *Mother Jones*. His research and perceptions about this case are reflected throughout this book. Thanks also to Cheryl Smith, who helped me decipher the workings of the polygraph, and Jan McInroy for combing through the manuscript with her careful eye.

Ann Close, my editor, and Wendy Weil, my agent, have been my invaluable companions and supporters for many happy years, and once again I acknowledge my gratitude for their advice and friendship.

REMEMBERING
SATAN

1

On the morning of Monday, November 28, 1988, the day that Paul R. Ingram was to be arrested, he dressed for his job, at the Thurston County Sheriff's Office, where he had worked for nearly seventeen years, went downstairs and ate breakfast, and then, to his surprise, suddenly vomited. He thought at first it must be the flu; then he realized that it was simply fear.

Ingram, who was forty-three, was already a familiar figure to most citizens of Olympia, Washington. Until that day, he had served as the chief civil deputy of the sheriff's department and the chairman of the local Republican party. He had been active in the deputy sheriffs' association and in the Church of Living Water, a Protestant fundamentalist congregation. He was the father of five living children. (A retarded daughter had recently died in a state institution.) As a politician, he was seen as a bridge between moderate conservatives and the Christian Right. As a police officer, he was more highly regarded by the public than by other police officers. Tall and square-jawed, with oversized glasses and a brown mustache, Ingram was known in his department for being a hard-ass type who enjoyed traffic patrol. Although Ingram claimed that he gave as many as five warnings for every ticket he issued, it is also true that he routinely made more stops than most officers. He developed a reputation for handing out speeding tickets for driving just five miles over the limit, and yet his personnel file contained not a single complaint; instead it was filled with commendations from citizens who wished to thank him for the courtesy he had shown while issuing their citations.

At eight o'clock that Monday morning, Ingram drove into the parking lot of the courthouse complex, which sits atop a hill beside Capitol Lake. Across the way, the white marble capitol looms, ghostlike, above the low-lying town, and beyond it one can see Budd Inlet, the farthest-reaching finger of Puget Sound. The briny air is full of the calls of seagulls, and the northern light is thin, even on a sunny day when the brooding Olympic Mountains are visible to the northwest and Mount Rainier shows off its snow-capped splendor fifty miles to the east. One can look at a map and imagine that the city is more vibrant than it actually is. The main highway on the western side of the state, Interstate 5, strings together Seattle and Tacoma, then reaches over to include Olympia before heading to Portland on its way to California. Olympia was once the largest port in the state, but with the decline of the timber industry the South Sound is virtually empty of maritime commerce. Neither the ferries nor the hydrofoils which course through the North Sound make a stop in Olympia. The city achieved a measure of regional fame through two local products that bear its name: the pale beer that is manufactured at the Olympia Brewery Company above the falls at the mouth of the Deschutes River, and the sweet, thumbnail-size oysters that grow in the bay. The brewery has long since sold out to Milwaukee interests; and as for the oysters, pollution and overharvesting have reduced them to an occasional, expensive delicacy.

Olympia became the capital of Washington Territory in 1853, when it was a bustling frontier outpost; now it is made up largely of bureaucrats, and the city bustles only when the legislature is in session. St. Peter's Hospital and a cardboard-box plant operated by Georgia Pacific are the other leading employers. Olympia is bordered by the townships of Tumwater and Lacey, making up what is known as the Tri-Cities, with a population of 68,000—Olympia proper accounting for just over half of that number. There are no skyscrapers, and parking is rarely a problem. Most people who live here like the slow pace, the modest scale, and the cozy society of small-town life. For many of them, the failure of the city to realize its early promise of becoming an industrial port like Tacoma or a sophisticated, international urban center like Seattle is a blessing that has allowed Olympia to stay charming and humane, if somewhat dull and self-satisfied.

Perhaps because of its beauty, its classical name, and a shroud of mystery that hangs over it—in the form of frequent fog or drizzle—Olympia has acquired a reputation as a spiritual center. J. Z. Knight, a well-known New Age channeler who owns a large estate off the Yelm Highway, is widely regarded as the richest woman in the county; the local lore is that her horse stables have chandeliers in every stall. Celebrity acolytes such as Shirley MacLaine and Linda Evans have sometimes passed through Olympia on their way to visit Knight. A small coven of witches runs a local herb shop. Like most Washingtonians, Olympians pride themselves on their tolerance in such matters, and it would be fair to say that the town is better known for its New Age believers than for its fundamentalist Christians; but both elements are deeply entwined with the life of the town, and are sometimes loudly at odds.

Fifteen minutes after Ingram arrived at work, he was summoned to the office of his boss, Sheriff Gary Edwards. An affable man with few enemies, Edwards was a rare Republican officeholder in a county long regarded as a stronghold of liberal Democratic politics. Ingram was not just an employee; he was an important political ally of Edwards and a friend for nearly a decade. In 1986 Edwards had appointed Ingram to be his chief civil deputy, causing some grousing on the part of those who had been leapfrogged by the junior officer; but Ingram had performed well in that position. He was better suited to administrative work than to investigations. Like Edwards, Ingram seldom gave offense; he seemed cheerful and unflappable—qualities Edwards had in abundance and which he apparently sought in his staff. With his earnest, friendly manner, Ingram was the kind of cop who was tailor-made for public appearances. He spent much of his time in schools talking to kids about the dangers of drug use, although he continued to do traffic patrol as he commuted to and from work.

Joining Edwards and Ingram in that meeting was the number two man in the department, Undersheriff Neil McClanahan. Intense and ambitious, McClanahan had risen through the ranks even more quickly than Ingram. They had known each other well since 1972, when both were young deputies and shared a county car. McClanahan wore glasses and a trim brown mustache, and when he put on his tweedy rain hat he bore a certain resemblance to Peter Sellers in the role of Inspector Clouseau—a point McClanahan would jokingly make about himself. It wasn't surprising that the careers of Paul Ingram and Neil McClanahan paralleled each other, since their skills and interests were similar; and although they were friends, they were also competitors in the small but still quite political hierarchy of the Thurston County Sheriff's Office. McClanahan's first action when he joined the other two men that morning was to relieve Ingram of the automatic pistol that he habitually wore in an ankle holster.

"Paul, there's a problem," Edwards said. He asked if Ingram knew about the charges of sexual molestation that his two daughters, Ericka and Julie, had made. (Ericka and Julie were then twenty-two and eighteen, respectively.) Ingram said that he did; however, he said he could not remember having ever molested his daughters. "If this did happen, we need to take care of it," Ingram said, but he added, "I can't see myself doing this." If he did molest the girls, then "there must be a dark side of me that I don't know about." These responses were disturbingly equivocal—a variation on the "maybe I did and maybe I didn't" theme that police often hear from suspects who are bargaining for a plea. But Ingram went on to say that if the charges were true, then not only his daughters but also his sons would need help. "I've never thought about suicide before, but if it turns out that I have done something, I want you to get all my guns out of the house, just in case," Ingram said, in a voice that sounded more puzzled than despairing. He requested a lie detector test, so he could "get to the bottom of this."

"I hope you're not going to make these girls go through a trial," Edwards said. The sheriff may also have been thinking of the reputation of his department, although at this very early stage in the investigation the prospect of a trial seemed remote. In fact, until this point, Edwards had confined the investigation to an administrative proceeding, such as might occur when citizens complain about an officer's erratic driving. An administrative inquiry might lead to a disciplinary hearing, which itself could result in a suspension or the loss of a job. It could all be handled very quietly.

Ingram willingly agreed to talk to investigators without a lawyer present, and so at nine a.m. McClanahan escorted him to the office of detectives Joe Vukich and Brian Schoening, who handled sex offenses. Both men knew Ingram well; in fact, his office was directly across the hall. Brian Schoening was a pale, sandy-haired veteran, a gravel-voiced grandfather with gray, unsurprised eyes. Ingram was the last man in the department that Schoening would have suspected of sexual abuse, but he had seen enough of the kinky underside of human nature to know that pleasant faces can hide appalling desires. Joe Vukich had met Ingram in 1976, even before joining the force;

after that they worked the same district, and Ingram had often invited the baby-faced rookie over to his house for barbecue and card games. As far as Vukich could tell, Ingram was a decent, easygoing family man and all-American husband. Ingram was both men's superior in the department; so from the beginning the interrogation was uncomfortable and conflicted for everyone, including the suspect.

Several hours into the questioning, Vukich turned on a tape recorder to take Ingram's official statement. Ingram now said, "I really believe that the allegations did occur and that I did violate them and probably for a long period of time. I've repressed it."

Vukich asked Ingram why he was confessing if he couldn't remember the violations, and Ingram replied, "Well, number one, my girls know me. They wouldn't lie about something like this. And, uh, there's other evidence."

"And what, in your mind, would that evidence be?" one of the detectives asked.

"The way they've been acting for at least the last couple years and the fact that I've not been able to be affectionate with them, uh, even though I want to be," Ingram said. "I have a hard time hugging them, or even telling them that I love them, and I just know that's not natural."

"Besides having a hard time being close to them, do you recall anything of a physical nature you may have done that could have been abusive, such as striking them?"

"Whew . . . I don't recall, uh, striking the girls," Ingram responded. "I don't lose my temper very often, but occasionally I do, or—or they may think that I'm, you know, arguing rather than, uh, conversing with them. Those may be looked at by them as abuse."

"If I asked you if you—and this is a yes-or-no answer—touched Julie inappropriately sexually, what would you say?"

"I'd have to say yes."

"And how about Ericka?"

"Again, I would have to say yes."

"What would you think the age of Ericka would've been when these things first started happening between you and her?"

"I can't recall myself, but I know that the age of five has come up in a couple of conversations." Ingram had first heard about the charges a week before.

"What do you remember?" the detectives pressed him.

"I don't remember anything."

It's not unusual in a police investigation for a suspect to say that he doesn't remember having committed a crime, especially if the crime is a sex offense. Oftentimes, the explanation involves the use of alcohol or drugs, but the claim of a faulty memory can also be a ploy on the part of the suspect to flesh out the charges—to see what evidence, if any, the police have. It was the experience of Schoening and Vukich that a suspect who said he didn't remember anything was either avoiding the truth or standing on the threshold of a confession; so at this point guilt was the tacit assumption that underlay the interrogation. Ingram wasn't saying "I didn't do it"; he was saying he couldn't *see* himself doing it.

Vukich turned off the tape recorder while he and Schoening attempted to move Ingram to accept his guilt. During the next twenty minutes, they told him that his daughters were shattered by his abuse, and provided him with some of the details that the girls had included in their statements. Ingram continued to be suspended between his statement that his daughters wouldn't lie and his assertion that he couldn't remember the abuse. He would later assert that Vukich assured him that the memories would return if he did confess (although there's no way to know if that assertion is true). According to notes that Schoening took during the interrogation, Ingram began praying feverishly. When the detectives turned on the tape recorder again, Schoening noted that Ingram was staring at the wall, clutching his hands, and that he then went into a "trance-type thing." Ingram began describing a scene in which he came into his older daughter's bedroom and removed his bathrobe. Then, he said, "I would've removed her underpants or bottoms to the nightgown."

"O.K., you say 'would've,' " one of the detectives said. "Now, do you mean 'would've,' or did you?"

"I did," said Ingram.

"After you pulled down her bottom, where did you touch her?"

"I touched her on her breasts and I touched her on her vagina. . . ."

"What did you say to her when she woke up?"

"I would've told her to be quiet and, uh, not say anything to anybody and threatened to her to say that I would kill her if she told anybody about this," Ingram said.

"O.K., you say you 'would've.' Is that 'would've,' or did you?"

"Uh, I did. . . ."

"And where did you go when you left her room?"

"I would've gone back to bed with my wife."

By the time the interview ended, many hours later, Paul Ingram had confessed to having sex with both his daughters on numerous occasions, beginning when Ericka was five years old. He had also talked about having impregnated his younger daughter, Julie, and taken her to have an abortion in the nearby town of Shelton when she was fifteen. All of these statements accorded in a general way with the charges his daughters had made, although Ingram's confessions were still maddeningly mired in conditional phrases. Brian Schoening, who is a talkative and emotional man despite his hard-bitten exterior, said later that he was deeply affected by Ingram's detachment in describing the sexual abuse of his daughters. Schoening had never seen such apparent remorselessness on the part of an offender, and it was even more galling to him because Ingram wore the same uniform that he did. Still, there was nothing very unusual about a community leader's being caught in a disgraceful act. If the case had ended that Monday, with Ingram's tentative confession, it doubtless would have caused only a brief sensation at most. In the ordinary course of things, he probably would have been spared a prison sentence and assigned instead to psychological counseling. His case would long since have been forgotten. But no one realized then where the hole in Ingram's memory would lead.

At four-thirty that afternoon, Ingram changed into the Thurston County jail's high-visibility orange coveralls and entered an isolation cell, subject to a twenty-four-hour suicide watch. Detective Schoening and Sheriff Edwards then made the dismal trip to Ingram's house in East Olympia to tell his wife, Sandy, the news.

2

The Ingrams owned ten acres off Fir Tree Road, near the Union Pacific Railroad tracks. Here the brief suburbs have grown ragged as the town turns into the country. There are rough houses and trailers and an abundance of powerboats and four-wheel-drive vehicles in the driveways. Scarcely a mile away is a corner of the immense Fort Lewis military reservation, which occupies much of the southeastern portion of the county. Occasionally, during maneuvers, one can hear the sounds of a mock war, with explosions and machine-gun fire. The house, which the Ingrams built in 1978, was not visible from the road. Although later it would be laden with spooky associations (McClanahan would compare it with the house in *The Amityville Horror*), on that November evening it was nothing more than an attractive barn-shaped structure, nicer than most homes in the area. It had the makings of a small estate. Both Paul and Sandy had developed a fetish for self-sufficiency. Paul raised chickens, rabbits, a couple of cows, and even ducks in a pond behind the house. A small herd of goats kept the lawn trim. Sandy maintained a year-round vegetable garden. A neighbor described the property as "well used," and it was indeed crowded with animal hutches and tools and a number of cars and trucks. For years Sandy had operated a day-care center in the house, so in addition to the normal clutter of family life the yard accommodated a swing set and a sandbox, and the house was full of plastic toys and rest mats.

Until that Monday, Sandy had thought of her marriage as happy, stable, and old-fashioned in a good sense. Paul's word was law, but because Sandy seldom disagreed with him, they almost never quarreled. She had her own life outside of the family—besides her day-care business, she had done a turn at public service, having spent one term on the county school board (in that sense, she was a more successful politician than Paul)—but for the most part her life was anchored in the home and the church.

Paul and Sandy had met in 1964, at Spokane Community College. Both were putting themselves through school, Sandy as a part-time maid and Paul as a janitor in a dairy plant. Both came from large and devout Catholic families. Sandy had spent two years in a convent school and had seriously considered becoming a nun. Paul had always attended Catholic schools and spent three years in a seminary, but he later decided that his priestly aspiration had largely been to please his mother. In any case, whatever clerical vocation he might have had melted away on the day he gave Sandy a lift to work. She was outgoing and full of fun, and they had so much in common. Paul was impressed that she was such a hard worker. Sandy also proved to be something of a tomboy; once, on a group outing, they went bobsledding down Mount Spokane on the hood of a '48 Buick, and Sandy laughed at the wild recklessness of it. Paul had practically no experience with girls; he rarely dated, and was a virgin when he met Sandy. They soon decided to marry, though both sets of parents were alarmed and thought they should wait. On their wedding day, in February 1965, both were nineteen years old. They had known each other for less than five months.

Paul's father, Sylvester, was a carpenter, an accountant, and a jack-of-all-trades who suffered from chronic ill health. His mother, Elizabeth, was a dietitian who held the family together during the hard times that followed a back injury to Sylvester in 1954. The children always had shoes and food, but little else. As the oldest of seven, Paul became the official baby-sitter and a virtual parent. His sister Robin recalls him as caring and self-sacrificing, and says he never expressed resentment at the extra burden he carried.

The family that Paul would help create resembled in many ways the family in which he grew up. Both of his parents were strict disciplinarians. Paul always felt that they showed much more love for each other than they showed for their children— a bitter observation that his own children came to echo. And however attentive and protective he may have been as an older brother, as a father Paul was a martinet, full of rules and prohibitions.

Sandy had been the youngest of four children and very much the family pet. She had a sweet, spunky disposition, and a stubborn streak that kept Paul from running over her. Although there had been a history of mental illness in her family, neither Sandy nor Paul worried about the possibility of a hereditary problem. Sandy, especially, wanted a large family; Paul wasn't so sure, but he didn't resist the idea. They set up housekeeping in a two-bedroom rented house in Spokane.

Paul Jr., also called Paul Ross by the family, was born in September of 1965, seven months after the wedding. With this new responsibility on his shoulders, Paul took a job as a building supervisor at a medical center. Months after Paul Ross's birth, Sandy learned she was pregnant again, this time with twins. Ericka and Andrea were born in September of 1966. Andrea, the firstborn, was underweight and sickly; Ericka was plump and healthy. Sandy took the younger twin home after a few days, but Andrea remained in the hospital for a week, and when she finally did come home she remained listless. The doctors assured Sandy that there was nothing wrong, Andrea was merely small; but a few days later she seemed to stop breathing. The panicked young parents rushed to the hospital with their gasping infant, who had turned blue as she struggled to breathe. Tests determined that she had spinal meningitis. A priest came to baptize her and administer the last rites, but Andrea confounded the doctors' expectations and survived. The meningitis, however, caused her brain to swell, with the result that her mental faculties were severely damaged and her skull was permanently enlarged.

The Ingrams quickly outgrew their little house. In early 1967 they bought, for $6,900, a three-bedroom house that had been repossessed by the Veterans Administration. The house was surrounded by a four-foot-high cyclone fence, which Paul Ross managed to scale while he was still in diapers. Sandy usually found him in the neighborhood, playing with other children, although twice she had to call in the police to locate him. From then on, he was kept on a leash when he played outdoors.

Paul hit the road, selling cameras door-to-door. It was his first real chance to travel, and he loved it, but the income never really covered their expenses. Sandy started looking after other people's children to take up the slack. Meanwhile, Andrea was in and out of the hospital with chronic attacks of pneumonia, and her needs became too great for the couple to handle. When she was still a baby, they sent her to a state institution, where she spent the rest of her life.

Sandy gave birth to a second son, Chad, in 1968. Paul, bowing to reality, took a more reliable job, as a field investigator with the Retail Credit Company. Later that same year, the company offered openings in several other cities. Moving would bring a pay raise and a chance for advancement. Paul and Sandy decided on Olympia, because it was small and semi-rural and appealed to their back-to-nature ideals. They bought a house trailer and moved it to the Flying Carpet mobile home park, in East Olympia. Soon Sandy was getting paid to look after other children in the camp. The income she provided was essential for the family, especially in those early days, but her own children came to feel that she paid more attention to the day-care children than to them.

Before long the expanding Ingram family was eager to move to larger quarters. When their fifth child, Julie, was born, in 1970, they secured a bank loan of $17,500 and built a three-bedroom house on a wooded lot in East Olympia. The boys shared one bedroom, and the girls shared another. Later they finished the basement, adding another bedroom and a recreation room. At last they had room for Sandy's garden and for the farm animals that Paul hoped would make them self-sufficient. He sold Amway products and a brand of dehydrated foods on the side. Shadowed by need throughout his own childhood, he was relentless in his drive to create security. From his point of view, he was being a good provider and giving his children an opportunity he had never had. But they began to feel that he valued them more as workers than as sons and daughters. "The old man didn't give a shit about anybody as long as you did your chores," Paul Ross later complained.

In 1969, almost as a lark, Paul applied to the reserve corps of the police department in Lacey, a small (there were only eight stoplights) adjoining township. He was accepted and began driving around in the evenings and on weekends with a borrowed pistol, doing traffic duty and handling domestic disputes. Within a few months he had learned enough about police work that he qualified to drive patrol on his own. Never in his life had he enjoyed anything so much. Paul thought of his police work as a hobby that brought in some additional money, but it also meant that he was spending almost no time at home with Sandy and the children. Chad had to teach himself how to ride a bike; later, he taught himself to drive a car as well.

In 1971, Paul moved from the Lacey Police Department to the Thurston County Sheriff's Office, and a year later the sheriff asked him to join the staff full-time. That meant a pay cut of a hundred dollars a month, which the family could scarcely afford; but Sandy supported Paul because he so obviously enjoyed the work. For the most part, Paul did well, although once in training class he made the mistake of offering his opinion that sheriffs should be appointed, not elected; the following morning he was invited into the chief deputy's office and thoroughly chewed out. The experience put him on guard about the politics of the office.

Paul quickly made friends in the department. He and Neil McClanahan, then another rookie, spent a lot of time together carpooling in the county car they shared. They often talked about religion, a subject of interest to both of them. At the time, Paul was still a Catholic, although he would eventually convert to a Protestant denomination; Neil was headed in the opposite direction. A deeply religious man, McClanahan was studying the catechism of the Catholic church and preparing for his own conversion.

Their spiritual pursuits and interest in civic service set them apart from most police officers, but neither man wanted to come across as a prude. Both joined a rotating poker game, along with several other deputies. Sometimes the game took place at the Ingrams' house. These games became so important to Paul that he installed a refrigerator in the basement recreation room to hold a keg of beer. No doubt, being a host to other members of the department, including the sheriff himself, enhanced Paul's standing and made him one of the guys. The morning after a poker party, the children would scour the floor under the table for loose change.

In 1972, Paul began having an affair with an older, divorced woman. Paul felt that he could discuss with her matters other than child rearing and the routine details of domestic life. His lover was a Lutheran, and she talked about her personal relationship with Jesus in terms that Paul had never heard in seminary. The affair foundered when it became clear that Paul would never leave Sandy. Although he was going to Mass less and less often, he was still enough of a Catholic not to believe in divorce.

Paul and Sandy's frugality, meanwhile, was paying off. They bought an old Ford pickup with a camper shell, and the family began spending summer vacations camping in Idaho. In 1976, they bought five acres of logged-off property on Fir Tree Road, with an option on an adjacent five acres. With characteristic energy, they began clearing the land in their spare time. Friends from the Olympia Police Department helped them put in a septic tank and grade a low spot into a pond. A nearby gravel pit provided material for a road at a bargain price. When carpenters finished the two-story house on the property, Paul and Sandy painted it together, inside and out. Jim Rabie, a detective in the Thurston County Sheriff's Office and a friend of Paul's, came to wire it, and Rabie's father built the kitchen cabinets.

At last, Paul and Sandy's dreams were realized. Their handsome home was surrounded by fir, alder, ash, cottonwood, cedar, and hemlock. In the spring, the dogwoods bloomed, and deer poked around in the bush. The woods were full of raccoons and possums and grouse, and there was an occasional red fox. There were ducks and herons in the pond. Sandy expanded her garden, making room for fruit trees and flowering plants. In addition to the chickens and rabbits that Paul raised, there was enough land to graze a few cows. It felt like paradise to Paul and Sandy, but not to their children, who thought of the place as remote and isolated.

The police investigators would interview many friends and neighbors of the Ingram family. Most described Paul and Sandy as ordinary folks who loved their children, even if they were strict. The most severe punishments meted out in the household included spanking for the younger children and being grounded for the older ones; usually it was a matter of withholding television or dessert. After the parents became devout fundamentalists, they didn't allow their children to participate in sports and rarely let them go to games or involve themselves in other extracurricular activities that might get in the way of chores or schoolwork. This was hardest on Chad, a natural athlete. "They weren't allowed to be kids," a neighbor observed, but the children always seemed well-mannered. Ericka and Julie were popular baby-sitters. One of the daughters' friends said that their dad was always yelling and that the brothers "goofed off and did weird things," although the only example of weirdness she could offer was that Chad had once tried to kiss her. A woman who had grazed a horse on the Ingram property said that Paul had called her and threatened to kill the animal if she didn't remove it right away. Every inch of his property had a purpose, he said; nothing was left for recreation.

The family doctor stated he had never seen any signs of abuse in the children. The Ingrams seemed healthy, for the most part. Ericka had a spate of heavy, irregular menstrual bleeding when she was sixteen, but that was common in the first three years of menstruation. Paul and Sandy belonged to a tennis club, and they played three times a week. At night, they all held hands and prayed before eating a big family dinner. The food was fresh, if somewhat rustic, although roasted rabbit and goat stew were not thought of as being terribly exotic in a region of the country where game was still a large part of the ordinary diet and self-sufficiency was held in high esteem. Sandy was always baking or stirring up something in the kitchen. She was a "perfect homemaker," said an admiring friend, who had once leased a trailer on the Ingram property. During that time the friend never observed anything unusual happening. Everyone who knew them described the Ingrams as a hardworking, Christian family; in fact, several people told the investigators that they had tried to model their own families on the Ingrams.

The previous year, Sandy had begun attending services at the Evergreen Christian Center, which is affiliated with the Assemblies of God. Paul was surprised, because Sandy had been deeply involved with their Catholic church, singing in the choir and teaching the catechism class. But he noticed a change in her right away—a softening, which he found very appealing. She began taking the children to the center on Sunday mornings and Wednesday nights. Eventually Paul went too, and he liked the open, welcoming atmosphere, although the hand waving and speaking in tongues put him off. A month later, however, Paul responded to an altar call and surrendered his life to Jesus. That fall, the entire family was baptized in the deep water.

The Ingrams were drawn to Pentecostalism in part because of its emphasis on the importance of the family. And yet, in the Ingram household, a troubling rift was developing between the parents and the children. Paul and Sandy were demonstrably affectionate with each other; indeed, there was a sexual charge between them that others could hardly miss. (They slept in the nude on a waterbed, and according to Paul they had sex nearly every other day.) With their children, however, they were stern and emotionally reserved. Sex was never discussed, except when the girls told Sandy that they intended to remain virgins until they married. There were few outlets for the children's emotional needs and youthful energy, however. Once the family joined the new congregation, Paul outlawed all sports activities and banned rock-and-roll music unless it was

Christian. Tensions worsened in 1978, when Sandy found herself pregnant again. After the child, a third son, named Mark, was born, Paul decided that he was going to make an effort to be a better father. Over time, the older children came to feel that Mark was their father's favorite; he was coddled rather than ordered around and put to work. Nearly every night, Paul read to Mark at bedtime—something that he had never done with the others—and later he bought the boy a computer and spent many evenings playing computer games with him. Ericka and Julie both complained that Mark was being spoiled.

The two older boys were rebellious and showed a disturbing tendency to live secret lives. In 1984, at the age of eighteen, Paul Ross turned down an appointment to West Point which his father had arranged, and then abruptly left home after wrecking his car for the third time in three months. He parked the car in a cemetery and left behind a note to Sandy saying that he had fallen in with a dangerous crowd. He warned his parents not to try to find him. "When you get this letter I'll probably be somewhere in South America," he wrote. Investigators later found the note in Sandy's desk. Their second son, Chad, whom Paul and Sandy considered the quietest and most even-tempered of their children, moved into an apartment in downtown Olympia for a short time during high school, and was arrested for shoplifting candy. Later, he went to Bible school in Tulsa, dropped out, and came back home to live.

Ericka and Julie, who shared a bedroom throughout their childhood, were often considered a pair, although Ericka was four years older than Julie and by far the more assertive. One can see a family resemblance: they inherited dark brown hair and eyes from both sides of the family, and have full, rounded faces, such as one might find in a portrait by Vermeer. What struck most people, however, was how different their personalities were. Ericka was moody and self-absorbed, Julie bubbly and outgoing, if somewhat in the shadow of her sister. Certainly Ericka was the beauty of the family, although she held herself apart and looked at life through eyes of cautious reserve. Her most striking feature was her mouth, which was small and sensual, with unusually high peaks on the arches of her upper lip; it was like the mouth of a Kewpie doll. She was still living at home when she turned twenty-two. Working as a tour guide at the capitol and intermittently attending college (she studied sign language and sometimes served as an interpreter for the deaf), Ericka always had her eye on the larger world. She bought stylish clothes and loved to travel. She had been to Greece, and in August of 1988 she had just returned from attending the Olympics in South Korea. Julie, on the other hand, was a homebody, like her mother. People thought she was the image of Sandy, and she dressed like her mother, in jeans and sweatshirts. Two years in a row, Julie had won the state championship in the Future Homemakers of America contest and had gone on to the nationals; that constituted most of her travel experience, except for the family vacations. The two girls were alike in one respect, though: they rarely went on dates—Ericka had been out only twice in the previous three years—and they were extremely shy around boys.

The Ingrams became a part of the extraordinary growth of Pentecostalism in America during the seventies and eighties. When the Evergreen Christian Center grew too large for the family's taste, they transferred to the Church of Living Water, an affiliate of the International Church of the Foursquare Gospel, which had been founded by the well-known evangelist Aimee Semple McPherson in the 1920s. The Church of Living Water was also growing quickly and soon moved from its modest quarters into an expansive campus with eight buildings that take up most of a city block. Like many congregations that once endured the stigma of being "Holy Rollers" on the poor side of town, the church projects an atmosphere that is intended to be informal and inviting. The sanctuary is a windowless theater called the Living Room, where the pastoral staff sit on a dais in easy chairs beside an artificial fireplace. It has the ambiance of the set of a daytime television talk show. There is a small gospel choir and a band.

Unlike the Catholic tradition that Paul and Sandy grew up in, the Pentecostal teachings of the Church of Living Water emphasized the truth of personal revelation, which sometimes appeared in dramatic forms. Here the congregation was often on its feet, waving its hands, shouting praise, instead of sitting in pews or kneeling silently at the altar rail. There was nothing rabid or fanatical about the services, as so many people still believed, but there was a powerful current of energy that could be shocking or thrilling, depending on what one thought about the message: that the Bible is the infallible word of God; that Jesus is His Son and will return to rapture the church and judge the world; that the only means of being cleansed from sin is through repentance and faith in Jesus; and that the gifts of the Holy Spirit—prophecy, healing, discernment, speaking or understanding strange tongues—are essential for personal salvation and available to all who believe.

The Ingrams were regulars at the church every Sunday morning and night and every Wednesday evening, and they also participated in the countless socials and study groups and retreats. Sandy started a food-and-clothing charity called Twelve Baskets, which became an important part of the church's community service. Frequently, Ericka would interpret sermons for deaf members of the congregation. She also persuaded her parents to take in two deaf girls as foster children, which proved to be an awkward arrangement for Paul and Sandy, because communication was so difficult.

The Church of Living Water sponsored an annual retreat for teenage girls called Heart to Heart, held at a camp on nearby

Black Lake. Julie and Ericka had attended for several years. Although she was really too old for the camp, Ericka returned in August of 1988 as a counselor. Five years earlier, during a fellowship discussion, Ericka had related an incident of what she characterized as attempted rape by a man she knew. The subject of sexual abuse sometimes arose during these sessions, and counselors took such revelations seriously. The authorities were alerted, and Jim Rabie, the sex-crime detective from the sheriff's office, followed up on Ericka's charge. He determined that there wasn't much substance to it—a married man had given Ericka a ride and put his hand on her knee—and the investigation was not pursued. Then, in 1985, during another Heart to Heart retreat, Julie said she had been sexually abused by a neighbor who lived on the Ingram property. When word of that charge got back to Paul, he took Julie to the county prosecutor and helped her file a complaint. Eventually, Ericka also accused the neighbor of improper sexual contact. Julie, however, became less and less able to speak about the alleged incident, to the point of becoming completely mute on the subject. Inconsistencies in her story began to surface, and the county prosecutor finally dropped the charges. Julie seemed relieved.

During the 1988 Heart to Heart, a woman from California named Karla Franko came to speak to the sixty girls in attendance. Franko is a charismatic Christian who believes she has been given the biblical gifts of healing and spiritual discernment. Before going to Bible college, she had been a dancer and a stand-up comic as well as an actress, and had parts in several sitcoms and TV commercials, which added a note of celebrity in the minds of the young girls in the audience. Often in speaking to youth groups such as this one, Franko would feel herself filled with the Holy Spirit and would make pronouncements that the Spirit urged upon her. Many extraordinary events took place at the 1988 retreat. At one point, Franko told the mesmerized group that she had a mental picture of a little girl hiding in a coat closet, and saw a crack of light under the door. Footsteps were approaching. There was the sound of a key locking the door. At that, a girl in the audience stood up, heaving with sobs, and cried out that she had been that little girl. Franko then had another vision. She said that someone in the audience had been molested as a young girl by a relative. Suddenly, a deaf girl rushed out of the room. A woman named Paula Davis, who, along with Ericka, was interpreting for the deaf campers, went after the girl and found her in the bathroom with her head in the toilet, trying to drown herself. In this charged atmosphere, a number of other girls came forward to say that they, too, had been abused. The counselors had their hands full.

Late in the afternoon of the last day of the retreat, the campers boarded buses to return to the church. Ericka remained in the conference center, sobbing disconsolately. She sat cross-legged on the floor of the stage with her head hanging between her knees. It was a dramatic, heartbreaking sight, but Ericka would not say what was wrong. The other counselors gave up trying to talk to her. They just gathered around her quietly to show their support. Finally, according to one of the counselors, she declared, "I have been abused sexually by my father."

"She seemed to be devastated just by having said those words," the counselor later told police.

Actually, that was only one version of the event—the version that the detectives placed in their files and later made available to defense attorneys. Another witness to the scene was Karla Franko, and she had a different account of what happened, which she claims she told investigators (there is no record of her statement in the files). Franko recalls that as she was getting ready to leave for the airport, a counselor came to her and asked her to pray over Ericka. "What does she need prayer for?" Franko asked. The counselor shrugged. Franko went back to the stage, where Ericka was sitting Indian-style, a portrait in dejection. Franko stood over her and began praying aloud. Almost immediately, she felt the Lord prompting her with information. She stepped back and was silent as she listened to the Lord's urgings. The word "molestation" presented itself to her.

"You have been abused as a child, sexually abused," Franko announced. Ericka sat quietly weeping, unable to respond. Franko received another divine prompting, which told her, "It's by her father, and it's been happening for years." When Franko said this aloud, Ericka began to sob hysterically. Franko prayed for the Lord to heal her. When Ericka's weeping eventually began to subside, Franko urged her to seek counseling, in order to get to the memories that were causing her so much pain. At no time, says Franko, did Ericka utter a word; she was so scathed and devastated by Franko's revelation that she could do little more than nod in acknowledgment.

Not long after the church retreat, both daughters abruptly moved out of the house. Ericka departed during the last week of September. She left the two deaf girls behind, in her parents' care. Julie left six weeks later. Both eventually moved in with friends, although Julie actually spent some nights sleeping in her car. Neither would say where they were or give any explanation for their actions. Paul and Sandy were distraught, especially about Julie. It was becoming a pattern in the Ingram household for the children to suddenly flee and hide, although Ericka, at twenty-two, had remained in the house longer than any of the others.

Ericka arranged to meet her mother after the evening church services the Sunday before Thanksgiving. That night there was an open house to dedicate the new sanctuary. Julie was there, and Paul took the opportunity to ask her to lunch. He said he wanted to talk about why she had moved out. Julie seemed to be in a cheerful mood and readily agreed. Paul then took ten-year-old Mark home, and Sandy went to meet Ericka at a nearby Denny's restaurant. She got there first, and sat at a table and ordered a cup of tea. For months, Sandy had sensed that Ericka was unhappy; but whenever she asked what was wrong, the only response Ericka had been able to give was a cryptic "You don't want to know." Now Ericka arrived in the company of her best friend, Paula Davis, who was to be her advocate in all that followed. Over the next two hours, Ericka talked of having been repeatedly molested by her father when she was young. In the last several years, she said, her brothers Paul Ross and Chad had molested her as well. Ericka linked her father's abuse to the poker parties in their old house. She said that the abuse had stopped when Paul was born again in the Pentecostal church, in 1975. As Ericka spoke, Sandy stared into her teacup. Finally she asked Ericka why she had never spoken about this before. "Mom, I did tell you," Ericka replied. "I tried to tell you, and you wouldn't listen."

"You're the only one in the family who didn't know," Davis added.

Sandy went home and confronted Paul. He said, "I never touched those girls." Chad was working late at the YMCA, and Sandy waited up for him. "You know I've always been a good boy, Mama," he said when she told him of Ericka's accusations against him. She called the associate pastor at her church, John Bratun, and learned that he already had heard about the allegations from the retreat counselors. According to Paul, Bratun told Sandy that the charges were probably true, because children didn't make up those kinds of things. Sandy and Paul had been planning to drive to the Oregon coast the next day for a week's vacation in a rented condominium, but that was now the last thing on Sandy's mind. In the morning, Sandy picked up Julie in the house where she was staying and drove her to school. On the way, Julie confirmed that her father and her oldest brother had molested her, too. She said that she had last been molested by her father five years earlier, when she was thirteen.

Against her better judgment, Sandy agreed to go ahead with the vacation, after her pastor said it would be good to get away. In her heart, Sandy felt that they should stay and deal with the accusations now, before they got out of hand; but Paul wanted to go—he needed to think. As soon as they left town, however, the investigation began in earnest. That very afternoon, a counselor from the local rape-crisis center took Julie to meet with police investigators, one of whom was Joe Vukich. The story she told them was somewhat different from the one she had told her mother that morning, and far more detailed. Julie said that the abuse had begun when she was in the fifth grade; her father was working the graveyard shift then, and sometimes he would sneak into the room where Ericka and Julie slept. He would be either naked or wearing shorts or sweats. He would get into bed with one of the girls and have vaginal or anal sex with her. As Julie told the story, she hid her face behind a curtain of brown hair. Each response came after a lengthy pause. Some questions she refused to answer. Because the investigators were concerned about the statute of limitations, which then extended for seven years in the case of assaults on minors, they concentrated on the most recent events. Julie told them that the last time her father had sexually abused her was three years before, when she was fifteen—not five years before, as she had told her mother. Detective Vukich asked Julie why she had never spoken to anyone about the assaults, and she replied that her mother had never wanted to listen.

That evening Vukich and Detective Paul Johnson, of the Olympia Police Department, interviewed Ericka at the home of a friend of hers from church. Vukich was immediately struck by how pretty Ericka was, and how vulnerable. She stated that her father had begun sexually abusing her when she was five years old. Vukich asked her to recall the last incident of abuse, and Ericka said she thought that she must have been in the fourth grade—well beyond the statute of limitations. Vukich kept pressing for more details. "Once, I felt like I hurt all over when I woke up—the bed was wet and yucky," Ericka said. Suddenly she burst into tears and ran into the bathroom. The detectives could hear her sobbing loudly for ten minutes. When she came back into the room, she said, "I caught a disease from my dad about a year ago. The doctor is in California, and also there is a doctor in Olympia who treated me." She now said that this 1987 incident was the last time she had sex with her father.

The detectives left at about midnight. With the testimony of two victims in hand, and with the promise of medical evidence, they already had a strong case to give to the county prosecutor.

Ericka called Karla Franko in California, and Franko expressed surprise at hearing from her. Ericka repeated some of the details she had given to Vukich and then informed Franko, "It is all coming down. They have Julie's confession." When Franko asked Ericka what she thought would happen to her father, she said he was going to lose his job. Given the fact that this was still an administrative proceeding, and not yet a criminal one, Ericka may have had reason to believe that the case would go no further than that.

Vukich interviewed Ericka again, during the Thanksgiving weekend. This time she said that the last incident of abuse had actually occurred during the final week of September, when she awoke to find her father kneeling beside her bed, touching her vagina. Vukich didn't question why she hadn't told him of this incident sooner; it's not unusual for victims of sexual abuse to make partial disclosures. But it was notable that in the space of one week both girls had assigned several different dates to the last incidence of abuse. In Ericka's case the time frame had moved from a decade earlier to a year earlier and then to just two months earlier.

Sandy tried to talk to Paul about the allegations while they were on vacation, but he was extremely reticent. He spent a lot of time reading his Bible and walking on the beach, but he had trouble composing his thoughts. He said he felt as if there were a solid mass of fear in his stomach, as dense and impacted as a bowling ball. Sandy stayed in the condo and cried. Paul assured her that nothing had happened, and Sandy believed him, but she was filled with dread. At one point, Paul suggested that the girls were trying to split them up, but neither he nor Sandy could imagine why their daughters would want to do such a thing.

And so when Sheriff Edwards and Detective Schoening knocked on the Ingrams' door that afternoon of Monday, November 28, and told Sandy that Paul had confessed, she went into shock. Her knees buckled, and she nearly fainted. She wobbled into the dining room and sat down at the table. Edwards and Schoening were afraid to leave her alone; she was so distraught that they feared that she, too, might consider killing herself. They got in touch with the Ingrams' pastor, Ron Long, and waited until Long and his associate John Bratun arrived. The last image that Schoening recalls of that night is of Sandy still sitting at that table, pale and stricken, with her pastors standing on either side. His heart went out to her. He was glad that he already had gathered up the weapons in the house.

Schoening had not known Sandy well until then, having met her only occasionally, at the sheriff's office annual Christmas parties and summer picnics, and he was surprised at how deeply her agony affected him. The contrast between Sandy's emotional collapse and Paul's puzzled detachment was especially distressing. It had been a long and troubling day; but Schoening found that this, unlike most cases he had handled, was one he couldn't leave at the office. That night, he had the first of a series of nightmares.

3

"COUNTY G.O.P. LEADER FACES
SEX-ASSAULT CHARGE," the front page of the *Olympian* pro-
claimed the next morning. The names of the victims were
withheld, in accordance with the newspaper's policy, but
Olympia is a small town, and anyone who wanted to know
the details had probably already heard them and had also heard
that the police were interviewing the children in Sandy's day-
care business, which she had immediately closed. In the chaos
of the moment, few who knew Sandy remembered that November 29 was her forty-third birthday.

Sheriff Edwards was well aware of the consequences of
seeming to protect one of his own—especially a political ap-
pointee whom he had jumped through the ranks and made
one of his chief deputies. Rather than turn the matter over to
another agency, however, Edwards decided to have his own
department conduct the investigation. He hoped to ward off
criticism by inviting a couple of detectives from other police
departments in the area to participate, while maintaining control in his own department. This decision would prove to be
the first of many mistakes. The Thurston County Sheriff's Office is a modest operation—at the time, 73 officers served a
county of 165,000 residents—and a personal crisis in one employee's family affected everyone else. No matter how objec-

tive Ingram's co-workers might try to be, their passions were instantly engaged. They felt surprised, embarrassed, and betrayed by their colleague. This was not merely one family's tragedy but a catastrophe for the morale of the whole department. To some extent, they, too, were victims in the case.

The investigative team Edwards put together included some of the best officers in the county. Every morning, and many afternoons, the team met in the conference room in the sheriff's office to discuss the case and divide up assignments. This room would become the scene of many agonizing debates. Seated around the table were Joe Vukich, dark and handsome but still baby-faced despite his mustache; Brian Schoening, who would fill the room with cigarette smoke and the washboard sound of his smoker's voice; Loreli Thompson, a detective who handled sex crimes for the Lacey Police Department; and, for a while, Detective Paul Johnson of the Olympia Police Department. As the investigation lengthened, Johnson dropped out; his department could not afford to lose him for months on end. Thurston County was small enough that every cop knew every other cop—by reputation, if not personally—and the detectives in this room represented the county's entire sex-crimes investigative force. They were used to cooperating with each other in special cases. An expert from the state patrol came in to help set up a computer program that could sort and classify the immense amount of data the detectives would eventually assemble. Overseeing the team was the most experienced investigator in the sheriff's office, Sergeant Tom Lynch, a tough and likable man who was head of detectives and would be the one person responsible for reading every bit of material and trying to make sense of it. Like Vukich and McClanahan—and Ingram, for that matter—Lynch had a dark mustache, the male cop's fashion statement.

Ordinarily, Lynch would have been in complete control of the investigation; but with the political implications of the Ingram case, and the public-relations problems posed by having a department investigate one of its own high-ranking officers, Undersheriff McClanahan unofficially took charge of the case. His usual duties were almost entirely administrative, so his active involvement was exceptional and seen by some in the room as unwanted meddling. McClanahan's perceptions of what occurred would shape and define the investigation, even though he only occasionally participated in the interrogations and rarely went into the field. He became the department's spokesman on the subject; and as the investigation deepened and broadened beyond what anyone could have imagined, he became more and more attached to the case. He had personal reasons for doing so: Ingram was a friend and a colleague (if also a rival), and McClanahan was perhaps closer to Ingram's family than anyone else on the force. He had felt a particular attachment to Julie when she was younger; he had always thought of her as his "little buddy." Ingram's revelations caused McClanahan to believe that his special relationship to Julie had filled a void in her life caused by her father's brutal breach of trust. (For her part, Julie did not remember having such a close relationship with McClanahan, but she came to accept that it must have been true.) Throughout the investigation, McClanahan saw his role on the team as being a voice for the victims.

On the morning after his arrest, Paul Ingram met with Richard Peterson, a Tacoma psychologist with a brusque, authoritative manner who often worked with the local police. Peterson would become an unofficial but highly significant member of the team. He first interviewed Ingram to determine his mental state and whether it was safe for him to be at large. As they talked about the case, Ingram asked why, if he had committed these heinous acts, he had no memory of them. Peterson told him that it was not uncommon for sexual offenders to bury the memories of their crimes because they were simply too horrible to consider. He went on to say that Ingram himself had probably been abused as a child. Peterson suggested that Ingram might recall being molested by an uncle, or even by his father. It would have happened when Paul was about five years of age, because that's how old his own children had been when he started to abuse them. Ingram said that the only sexual memory he could dredge up from his early childhood was his mother's cautioning him not to scratch his crotch in public. According to Ingram, Peterson then assured him that once he confessed, the repressed memories would come flooding back (although, once again, there's no way of establishing that as fact). But he had confessed already, Ingram said, and he didn't remember any more today than he had remembered yesterday. Peterson didn't have an answer for that; however, Ingram asked if he would attend the afternoon interrogation with Schoening and Vukich—perhaps Peterson could unblock whatever it was that was keeping him from remembering.

That day Vukich acquired two letters that Julie had written to a teacher, Kristi Webster, five or six weeks before. Webster had noticed a profound change in Julie's behavior in the fall of 1988. The eager, hardworking student Webster had known the previous semester had become morose and distracted, dragging through her classes with a haggard and blank face. Along with a friend, Julie had gotten in trouble for making long-distance calls from a school telephone. Julie had never broken a rule before, and so Webster asked her to write a note explaining why she was misbehaving. Julie wrote:

> My feelings about this whole ordeal are totally weird. Sometimes I feel good and sometime bad and then there are the day I feel totally confused and just wish I could move to a different state and start life all over w/ new friend and no one would have to know about my past. And I have time

mostly at night when I'm so scared. I don't sleep I just wait in my room for my *dad*. I hate it. I will never enjoy sex. It hurt so bad and it makes me feel very dirty.

Being a Christian I suppose to forgive *him* for what he did and still does to me, but Its very hard he also says thing to me like "if your a good girl God will take care of you." And if you tell you'll pay for it I promise you.

The significant statement in this part of the letter was that the abuse was still occurring at the time it was written. What followed, however, was even more explosive and changed the course of the investigation entirely. For Julie's memory now implicated people other than family members:

> I can remember when I was 4 yr old he would have poker game at our house and alot of men would come over and play poker w/ my dad, and they would all get drunk and one or two at a time would come in to my room and have sex with me they would be in and out all night laughing and cursing. I was so scared I didn't know what to say or who to talk to. The wierd thing was Ericka & I shared a room and they never touch her because she would *say* something and also at night most the time she slept on the top bed. And I think my dad & all his friend were afriad the bed might break. And my dad was always said to them Stay away from her (Ericka). She is under special care of her doctor and he will find out.

A sex ring of pedophiles would in itself be earth-shaking news in Thurston County, but Vukich realized that the letter was even more incriminating than that. He knew about the poker games—Ericka had mentioned them in her confrontation with her mother—but he also knew that most of the poker players were colleagues of Ingram's at the sheriff's office. Tom Lynch, the chief of detectives, had been a regular at the games; so had Undersheriff McClanahan; even Vukich had sat in occasionally. The game had seemed to him completely innocent. Had it all been a charade, a front for a conspiracy of sex criminals operating out of the Thurston County Sheriff's Office?

Julie's second letter to Kristi Webster revealed the degree of her despair:

> I am so freaked out I can't even eat I have so much going through my head. It's very hard to understand. I'm really scared about this whole situation I don't know if I doing what is right I feel like this is all my fault that I cause this to happen I'm the problem and I wonder what going to happen to my family will my dad be lock up and my mom left behind w/ Mark or will this just blow over and no one will understand where I'm coming from. I'm at the edge of my rope.

Despite the fact that much of the department and key members of the investigative team had been implicated in the case, Vukich and Schoening renewed their interrogation of Paul Ingram that afternoon. The psychologist Richard Peterson joined them and quickly took control of the interview. He must have felt like a prophet; even before the interview officially began, Ingram confided that he was beginning to remember being abused by his uncle, as Peterson had suggested only that morning.

First, however, Ingram wanted to clear up the confusion he felt about being interrogated by his fellow officers. He had been crying and praying in his cell, and he expressed his anxiety that Schoening and Vukich doubted his sincerity. "I really want you to—to believe that I'm telling you the truth."

"Why is that important to you?" Peterson asked.

" 'Cuz I don't think Brian believes me," said Ingram.

"Their job is not to believe you," Peterson said bluntly. "It's to try and get as much information as possible."

"And I'm trying to—to prove that I am being cooperative," Ingram stuttered. "There's—I—I'm—I truly am."

Schoening responded in the same personal, emotional vein. "I guess what my feeling is . . . even this morning we gained some additional information, from Julie, okay, and I guess what I'm saying is . . . she has a good reason to suppress this crime—more than you do, Paul. I mean, this has really happened to her."

What troubled Joe Vukich is that Ingram was a cop, "and as cops we have a very factual, very punctual, very data-minded frame of reference, if you will."

"Uh-huh," Ingram agreed.

"And that's what makes it hard for us at least to comprehend that you can't recall this, because I'll bet you could go back and take a citation you wrote ten years ago . . . you'd pretty much remember what happened that day."

"Yeah, you're probably right. In a lot of cases I could do that."

"That's what confuses me about this," Vukich continued. "What happened with Julie happened just last month. It's—it's very real, it's very recent. Granted, it's very hard to talk about."

"I can't see it," Ingram protested. "I can't visualize it in my own mind."

"Your wife called this morning and tells me that Chad is really, really upset and shook about all this and he wants to talk to me as soon as he can," said Schoening. "What all he'll have to say I don't know, but it sounds to me like we're probably talkin' about all four of your kids, maybe all five of 'em. Your wife is sittin' there telling me how she can stand by ya and still love ya. I don't know why she should. . . . You're just tryin' to keep from tellin' any more than you have to tell. . . . It's kinda like a nonadmission admission."

Peterson began asking Ingram to describe his sex life with Sandy, which Ingram did with some enthusiasm.

"Did you ever use alcohol as part of your lovemaking?" Peterson asked.

"No, I—it would seem to me that alcohol would sting," Ingram said, surprised.

"It was pointed out that you used to drink quite a bit," Peterson said, making himself clear. "Someone said you used to have quite an appetite for beer."

"Oh," said Ingram, "what I would do . . . we got an old refrigerator and put a keg of beer [in it] and we used to have poker parties at the house and I did like to come home after I'd been workin' swing shift and sit down and have one, uh, maybe two beers."

Now that he had mentioned the poker parties, the questioning became more focused. "Would you drink more then?" asked Schoening.

"I can't say I never got intoxicated," said Ingram. "But I can remember, you know, some of the guys getting pretty wasted, and over a period of four or five hours I might have four beers."

"Where was your wife during the poker parties?" asked Peterson.

"As I recall, she would've gone to bed, 'cuz we'd stay up and play pretty late."

"So the poker buddies that you played with would be who?" asked Peterson. "Friends from the department, or—"

"Yeah, most of 'em were friends from the department, or friends of theirs," Ingram agreed. "We'd get, I don't know, five or eight guys together." He then named several men, most of whom were police officers. There were two names he failed to mention, a fact that would soon become significant.

"One night I won over a hundred dollars, and my wife

said, 'Hey, that's wrong,' and I said, 'Okay, I'll play next weekend and lose it all,' " Ingram related. "The next weekend we played and I couldn't lose for tryin'. It was unreal. I won about a hundred twenty-five dollars, and we just quit."

"Were the kids aware of the poker parties?" asked Peterson.

"Oh, yeah, 'cuz we played underneath their bedrooms."

"Anybody go up to see the kids?" asked Vukich.

"I just can't think of anything where anybody—"

"The reason I ask, Paul, is because Julie told me about a time or two where when there was a poker party she was molested."

"What we're talking about, Paul, is she was molested by somebody other than you," Schoening clarified in his rumbling voice. "She even remembers being—somebody tying her up on the bed and two people, at least, taking turns with her while somebody else watched, probably you."

Ingram gasped in surprise. "I just don't see anything," he said when Schoening pressed him. "Let me think about this for a minute. Let me see if I can get in there. Assuming it happened, she would've had to have had a bed, bedroom by herself . . . uh . . . ."

The pauses in Ingram's statement sometimes lasted ten full minutes, intensifying the frustration on the part of the questioners. He would grab hold of his hair and lean forward, dead still, until his limbs went to sleep, while the investigators stood around, fuming with impatience. Schoening prodded Ingram by saying that even as they talked Julie was in fear for her life. "That person is still out on the street. That person is some friend of yours that worked or works for this department."

Schoening's remarks would have serious consequences, so it's important to note the assumptions buried in them. Julie's fears, insofar as she had expressed them, were about whether she was doing the right thing in coming forward with her story, and whether she would break up her family as a result. The only person she had seemed to be afraid of was her father. There was nothing in the record at this point that reflected her terror of being stalked by a potential killer. The extrapolations about her fear of someone else were only guesswork on Schoening's part. The terms of the investigation had been redefined, however.

"We need to protect her, Paul," warned Vukich.

"She's terrified, Paul," Schoening added.

"I—I hear what you're sayin', but just be quiet and let me think," Ingram pleaded.

"Apparently, it's somebody that's still close to you, Paul," said Schoening, once again departing from the record. Was he guiding Ingram toward some private judgment of his own?

"Jim Rabie played poker with us. Jim and I have been fairly close," Ingram said helpfully. James L. Rabie, the man who had done the electrical work on the Ingrams' house as a favor, once worked sex crimes. As a matter of fact, he had been the one who had investigated Ericka's prior claim of attempted rape and had decided it wasn't worth pursuing. At that time, he held the job that Schoening had now, that of senior investigator. Rabie and Schoening had a long-standing and well-known dislike of each other. Ingram had not mentioned his name in his original list of poker players.

"Is Jim the person she's talking about?" Vukich asked.

"Just—just don't put words in my mouth," Ingram responded. "Jim has some—I guess I'd say—what I consider to be unnatural sexual attractions."

"What do you mean by that?"

"We went over to Yakima one time for something, and Jim bought some magazines, said to help him in his job when he was doing sex crimes. And he looked at 'em. I didn't. I just don't do that kind of thing. . . . Geez, I'd hate to think he'd had anything to do with my kids."

"How would you feel if he did?"

"Anger—uh, bitterness comes in. I just, gosh . . ." Ingram went quiet for a moment. "I'm trying to get—to bring something up here. Uh . . . uh . . . Jim's the only one that comes to mind. . . ."

"In this picture you have, Paul, do you see ropes?"

"Uh, you've put the ropes there, and I'm trying to figure out what I've got," said Ingram. "It kind of looks to me like she'd be lying facedown . . . kind of like she's hogtied."

"What else do you see? Who else do you see?"

"Maybe one other person, but I—I don't see a face, but Jim Rabie stands out, boy, for some reason."

Schoening went out in the hall to collect himself. Sergeant Lynch saw him there. Schoening appeared so agitated that Lynch relieved him of his gun. "It's not Paul Ingram I want to kill," Schoening told him. "It's Jim Rabie."

As Schoening walked back into the office where the interrogation was taking place, he passed Peterson coming out, his eyes streaming with tears. Peterson, so gruff, so schooled in the cruel twists of the criminal and the insane mind, had been emotionally overpowered, not only by the scenes of bondage that Ingram was describing but also by Ingram's infuriating detachment. Vukich, too, had tears in his eyes. But Ingram sat calmly, and he grinned in greeting when Schoening came back in. Schoening had never seen anything like this monstrous equanimity.

"Paul, have you ever had any sexual relations with Jim Rabie?" Schoening asked.

"I don't think so," Ingram said, in that same puzzled tone that was becoming unbearable for the interrogators. "I'd just hate to think of myself as a homosexual."

"Did I hear you say that you offered your wife to Jim?" Peterson said as he came back in the room, apparently misunderstanding the gist of the conversation.

"That I offered my wife?" Ingram asked. "No, I . . .

Number one, my wife would—I don't want to say she'd kill me, but she'd come close to it."

"Have you ever had any affairs at all, Paul? Extramarital affairs?" Schoening asked.

Ingram admitted that he had had an affair. "It was right about the time Julie was born."

This line of questioning had long since left the track of the original question of sex abuse. Without a lawyer present, the detectives and the psychologist were firing in all directions, hoping to hit some as yet unspecified target.

"Have you ever worn any of your wife's undergarments?" asked Schoening.

"I don't think so," Ingram replied. "I'd say no."

"Have you ever done any peeping?"

Ingram vividly recalled that, when he was working as a supervisor for a cleaning crew at Seattle First National Bank, every evening a woman across the street would undress in front of her window. "I'd stand up in the second-floor window and watch her," Ingram said. "She did a little dance. It got to the point that all the women were watchin' her, too. Finally somebody complained and the police made her close the blind."

"Why do you think you remember some of this stuff pretty well and . . . don't remember about your sons and daughters?" asked Schoening.

Ingram said he didn't know.

"Do you think it's because that involvement with your sons and daughters is illegal and it's hard for you to admit to that?" asked Vukich.

"More than illegal," said Ingram. "In my mind it's immoral and unnatural."

"Have you ever influenced or watched or had anything to do with your sons molesting your daughter?" asked Schoening.

"I don't have a picture, and that's the only way I can describe it to you."

That question would prove to be significant later in the case, as would one that soon followed, from Dr. Peterson, who asked, "Before your conversion to Christianity, were you ever involved in any kind of black magic?"

Ingram replied that there was a time when he had read his horoscope in the newspaper. "I don't know what you're driving at," he added.

"The Satan cult kind of thing," Schoening said.

This was the first mention of satanism in the Ingram case. Later, the detectives claimed that Ingram had previously brought the subject up himself, but it's obvious that in this exchange he did not pick up the theme—at least consciously. All Ingram could recall was that as a child, on Halloween, he had tied a cat in a sack and hung it from a telephone pole.

Over the next hour, Schoening, Vukich, and Peterson changed their strategy. They began to concentrate on Ingram's guilt. The mood began to change. "Do you know how badly damaged your daughter is?" asked Peterson, referring in this instance to Julie. "Eighteen years old, she's a senior in high school, and she can't look at wedding things. . . . She thinks she's responsible for destroying your family."

"That she's dirty," said Schoening.

"She shakes at the thought of having to talk about this stuff," Peterson continued. "She's frightened of you."

"And she's frightened of whoever this other person is," Schoening added, once again hypothesizing.

"She can't name the other person?" asked Ingram. "I don't want to put her through this, don't get me wrong."

"You're putting her through it by not recalling," said Peterson.

"Yeah, you are, Paul, 'cuz right now she's havin' a difficult time talkin' about it," said Schoening. "You gotta help if you want this stopped or you may have either a suicidal daughter or a dead daughter. . . . She can't take much more of this,

Paul. I mean, it's all comin' back to her and she's havin' a real difficult time."

"Oh, Lord."

"I've got some notes here," said Peterson. "When she was having her period, she says you put your penis in her butt. Did you hear that? Anal sex with your daughter."

"My kids always tell the truth," Ingram replied.

"Why don't you listen to what she wrote here, Paul," said Vukich. "She says, 'I was four years old, he would have poker game at our house and a lot of men would come over and play poker with my dad and they would all get drunk and one or two at a time would come into my room and have sex with me.' Now, your daughter wrote that."

"This is her writing, Paul," echoed Schoening.

"And you told us that she's honest," said Vukich.

"Oh, yes, my kids are honest." Ingram was sobbing now.

"So it's time, Paul," said Schoening. "Quit beatin' around the bush and let's get this out."

Everyone in the room sensed that they were on the edge of a breakthrough. Between the tears, Ingram prayed aloud. He asked that his pastor be called.

"It goes back to the poker games, Paul," Vukich reminded him as Ingram closed his eyes and began rocking violently back and forth.

"Choose life over living death," Peterson exhorted, lapsing into the religious language that seemed to reach Ingram. "You are as alone as Jesus was in the desert when he was comforted."

"God's given you the tools to do this," Vukich said. "You've got to show him by what you do and what you say as to whether or not you're worthy of his love and redemption and salvation."

"Oh, Jesus!" Ingram cried in a frenzy. "Help me, Lord! Help me, Lord!"

"One of the things that would help you, Paul, is if you'd stop asking for help and just let yourself sit back, not try to think about anything," Peterson said, in a tone that was suddenly quiet and calming. "Just let yourself go and relax. No one's going to hurt you. We want to help. Just relax."

In response, Ingram instantly went limp. He hunched over and put his face in his hands.

"Why don't you tell us what happened to Julie, Paul?" Vukich said. "What happened at that poker game?"

"I see Julie lying on the floor on a sheet. Her hands are tied to her feet. She's on her stomach," Ingram said. His voice was high and faint. There was no doubt in anyone's mind that he was in a trance. "I'm standing there looking at her. Somebody else is on my left."

"Who is that?"

"The only person that keeps coming back is Jim Rabie."

"Turn and look at that person," Schoening said.

"He's standing right next to you, Paul," Vukich said. "All you have to do is look to your left and there he is."

"He's—he's standing up," Ingram said. "I see his penis sticking up in the air."

"Does he have any clothes on?"

"I don't think so," said Ingram. He then mentioned the name of another sheriff's deputy who might also be in the room. For some reason, the investigators had no interest in this other man.

"Go back to that person who's standing there with his penis sticking up in the air, Paul," said Schoening. "What's he doing to your daughter?"

"Getting down on his knees," said Ingram. "He's behind my daughter."

"Is he puttin' his penis in her?"

"Uh, her legs are close together, but maybe she's being rolled over onto her side."

"What she saying, Paul?"

"She's saying no. . . ."

"He's rolling her over," said Vukich. "What's happening next?"

"She can't go over on her back 'cuz her legs and her hands are there. It looks like she might have something around her mouth."

"A gag?"

"Like a gag," Ingram agreed.

"Who put that on her?"

"I might have. I—I don't know. . . ."

"Is she clothed or unclothed?" Peterson asked.

"Unclothed, I believe. . . ."

"What's this person doing?"

"He's kneeling. His penis is by her stomach. Uh, he's big. I mean, broad-shouldered, big person."

"Any marks on his back?"

"He's hairy."

"Does he have any jewelry on?" Vukich asked.

"May have a watch on his right hand." Rabie is left-handed and wears his watch on his right hand.

"What time does it say?"

"Uh, two o'clock."

"How close are you to him?" asked Peterson.

"I'm pretty close."

"How are you dressed?"

"I don't think I've got anything on."

"Do you have an erection?"

"I think so. . . ."

"Are you rubbing yourself against her?"

"Uh, yes. . . ."

"Is somebody taking pictures?" Vukich asked.

"Uh, pictures—is there somebody off to the right of me? Uh, it's possible, let me look. I see—I see a camera."

"Who's taking the pictures?"

"I don't know. I don't see a person behind the camera."

"That person's very important," Peterson said. "He's the one that holds the key. . . ."

"Well, the person that I think I see is Ray Risch," Ingram said. Raymond L. Risch, Jr., was a mechanic who worked for the Washington State Patrol.

This interview lasted until late in the evening. John Bratun, the associate pastor of the Church of Living Water, arrived after dinner in response to Ingram's request, as did Gary Preble, an attorney, whom Ingram had also asked for. Ingram knew Preble through the local Republican party. Preble was a devout charismatic Christian, but he had practically no criminal experience and certainly had no idea that he was about to take on the biggest case in Thurston County history.

The little office where the interrogation took place became stale and overheated from the press of so many bodies. "Boy, it's almost like I'm making it up, but I'm not," Ingram said as the interview drew to a close. He had now implicated several people in addition to Jim Rabie and Ray Risch. He had produced several new memories of sexual abuse, one occasion as recent as the week before he left on vacation. He had also begun to see "weird shadows" and tombstones. "It's like I'm watching a movie," he told the detectives. "Like a horror movie."

4

Thursday, December 1, was a busy day for Jim Rabie. For the past year he had been working as a lobbyist for the Washington State Law Enforcement Association and serving as the lieutenant governor of the state Kiwanis organization. That day Rabie had three Kiwanis meetings in three different cities, beginning early in the morning and not finishing until late that night. By mid-afternoon he was exhausted. He suffers from narcolepsy and usually requires two naps a day to keep himself going; in fact, that disease, and his tendency to fall asleep at inopportune moments, had caused him to retire from the sheriff's office in 1987, after fourteen years in the department.

Rabie was a sociable type with a plump face and sleepy eyes. At the age of forty-five, he still had dark and curly hair. Although it was not really detectable, one leg was an inch and a half shorter than the other one, the result of a car wreck when he was a child, and he wore a built-up shoe. He didn't limp, but he couldn't move around very quickly. Most people who knew him thought of Rabie as a pleasant, decent fellow who liked a joke and usually wore a smile.

At three o'clock he stopped by the office of his insurance agent to pay off a bill. He asked the agent, who was a friend, if he had heard about the arrest of Paul Ingram. Rabie himself had gotten the news from a source in the department. He was dumbfounded, he told the agent, because Paul was such a close friend—Ingram had been Rabie's best man at his wedding, and Rabie had been Ingram's campaign manager when he made a losing bid for the state legislature, in 1984. "It just goes to show you, child abuse can happen anywhere," Rabie said.

The agent remarked that it must be frightening for a cop to face prison. Rabie said that the machinery of law enforcement had to be very careful when arresting a police officer, and for that reason he thought that the case against Ingram must be compelling. But he was puzzled by the fact that Paul seemed to be "playing games" with the investigators. When Rabie himself was investigating sexual abuse, a suspect who confessed was usually given a "safe to be at large" evaluation and let out of jail after a day or two. A suspect who was not cooperative was probably "in denial," Rabie said. Such a person would be sent to a state institution for evaluation and faced a likely prison sentence. As a cop, Ingram would know this.

The two men then talked about other cases of abuse and agreed that in most such cases the perpetrators were people who themselves had been abused as children. Often the abuse was completely blocked out of active memory and would come to light only when a person entered therapy later in life for some sexual concern, such as frigidity. It was for that very reason, said Rabie, that he lobbied successfully to get the statute of limitations changed in the state of Washington so that the perpetrator of a sex crime against a minor could be held liable for seven years, rather than three. (Later, the law was amended again, to allow charges to be brought for three years after a victim *remembers* a crime. It was a pioneering statute and has since been replicated by twenty-two other states.)

The agent decided to take a break and smoke a cigarette, so he walked outside with Rabie. The two men stood on the sidewalk shooting the breeze. Later, the agent would try to reconstruct the conversation, which at the time seemed interesting but certainly not consequential. He remembered that Rabie said that Joe Vukich was the investigating officer and that Vukich might "go too deep." It was a mistake to try to get all the details of a crime, many of which wouldn't be needed to gain a conviction. Rabie also mentioned that he had "an affinity" for abusers. He understood how they felt. It was that very quality, Rabie believed, that had helped him elicit confessions.

When the agent finished his cigarette, he went back to work, and Rabie drove over to the County Seat Deli, a cozy spot across the street from the courthouse complex that was always full of lawyers, judges, deputies, clerks, and secretaries who work at the county offices. At five o'clock he was meeting his wife, Ruth, and his friend Ray Risch for a bite to eat.

Risch, who was forty-one in 1988, was six feet four and thin, with a dark beard. He wore tortoiseshell glasses that were always sliding down his nose, and he had a shy habit of laughing and looking up and away—an oddly demure gesture in such a large man. He never seemed to know what to do with his long limbs, so when he was relaxing he had a way of crossing his arms and wrapping his legs around each other at the knee and ankle, like vines. When round Jim Rabie and gangly Ray Risch were together, one couldn't help thinking of Laurel and Hardy. Everyone who knew them would remark that Rabie and Risch were pals; they met for lunch nearly every day and often got together for dinner with their wives. Both were avid readers and like to work on cars. Rabie was the talker. Risch liked to listen and laugh.

The table talk, of course, was about their friend Paul Ingram. Ruth Rabie was a corrections officer in the Thurston County jail, where Ingram was being held. A firm, quiet grandmother who was looking forward to retirement, Ruth had been married to Jim for nearly twelve years. They had met when she joined the women's reserves in the sheriff's department. As a jailer, Ruth privately worried that Ingram was going to do something crazy that would cause him to be killed. This was just a wild and irrational thought, since Ingram was on suicide watch and being carefully monitored, but it was so strange having a friend and a high official in the sheriff's office suddenly behind bars.

Jim said that earlier he had called Sandy to ask if there was anything he could do. "How could this have been going on and me not know it?" she had asked him plaintively. He didn't know what to say. In his experience, he had found that many awful things could go on in a family without being acknowledged, even by the victims.

"There are two Paul Ingrams," Ray Risch said enigmatically. Jim asked what he meant by that. Ray said that every police officer has two personalities: one the ordinary civilian guy, the other the authoritative person behind the badge. The same was true of Jim when he was in the department, Ray observed.

Rabie and Risch didn't know at the time that either of them was under suspicion; but even as they were talking, Ingram was across the street in the interview room producing new memories of their having molested his children. That very morning, Julie had picked their faces out of a photo lineup and had described an incident in which, during one of the poker games, Rabie came into her room, raped her, and cut her with a knife.

When they finished chatting at the deli, Rabie went to another of his Kiwanis meetings and then drove across the street to return a slide projector to the sheriff's office; he had borrowed it from the crime-prevention department, which Paul Ingram headed. Since no one had ever asked Rabie to return his office key when he retired, he simply unlocked the back door and walked in. It was after seven. Rabie was wearing his red Kiwanis blazer. In the hallway, he saw Tom Lynch walking into the small room that Schoening and Vukich shared. Rabie stuck his head in to say hello. The detectives looked startled.

"What are you doing here?" Lynch asked.

"Returning this," said Rabie. "I'm a little surprised to see you here this late."

He wasn't nearly as surprised as they were.

"Can I ask a question?" Rabie continued earnestly, taking a seat in the same chair that many suspects had sat in when Jim Rabie was a detective in this very office. "I know that possibly you guys can't answer it, but has Paul been honest? I mean totally honest, because unless he is he will not be amenable to treatment." Obviously, Rabie was presuming Ingram's guilt. According to Lynch's notes, Rabie then said, "Paul and I have been very close for a long time, and maybe it would help if I talked to him."

There was a long, awkward pause. It was so bizarre, having a suspect breeze right into the sheriff's office, although weirdness had been a part of this case from the very beginning. The sense of unreality was heightened because Ingram and Rabie were so well known in the department. An unsettling feeling of identity tied the detectives to the suspects. Indeed, if Rabie had not retired, he would have been in charge of the case, so there was an odd, mirrored quality of investigators investigating the investigators. Finally, Schoening broke the silence and told Rabie, "You've been named."

Instead of immediately and adamantly denying the charge, Rabie undid his tie and sat back in the chair with an immense sigh. Vukich and Schoening exchanged a look. They identified this as the "Oh, no, I've been caught" reaction.

Rabie's initial response seemed to them eerily similar to Ingram's. He said that he couldn't remember the events he was being charged with, and he speculated that perhaps he had a "dark side." Also like Ingram, Rabie asked several times to take a polygraph exam. At nine-thirty that evening, Schoening turned on a tape and read Rabie his rights. Rabie also agreed to talk without a lawyer present. "I am completely baffled by what in the devil is going on," Rabie said.

"Jim, you're doin' the same exact thing to us tonight that you have seen with probably hundreds of pedophiles," Schoening said impatiently. "They want to minimize; they want to deny."

"I agree," said Vukich.

"Individual people, separately, have corroborated that you masturbated in front of and on Julie. Julie tells us that; so does Paul Ingram tell us that," Schoening continued, selecting one of various conflicting stories. "Don't you think you're in a denial stage?"

"I must be, because I honestly do not have any recollection of that happening, and I do not believe that I could've done it and blocked it out."

"How do you feel right now?"

"In a daze," said Rabie. "Scared."

"What're you scared of?"

"Because I know from your end of it that if you've got what you tell me you have, that I'm not leaving here. I'm gonna be in custody. And I have a firm belief that any cop that's charged is guilty until proven otherwise."

Vukich asked what Rabie would think if he were sitting on the other side of the desk with the same information. "What would be your honest evaluation?"

"Same things you're thinking," Rabie admitted. "That I must be guilty, and that I must be in a denial state." The significance of his plight swiftly settled in on him. "An ex-cop in prison is almost a sign of death," he observed. Even if he got off, the mere fact that he had been charged would mean that his reputation was destroyed, his lobbying career was finished, his Kiwanis work was over, his marriage was placed in peril, and he might not be allowed ever to see his granddaughters again, because suspicion that he was a child molester would always hover around him. In short, his life was ruined.

"I can't figure out why, if I did this, I wouldn't remember it happening," Rabie said, echoing Paul's complaint.

"You can't admit it to yourself, Jim, that's the problem," said Schoening. "You're like Paul was. You can't convince yourself that you really could have been part of this."

"I can't even picture someone masturbating on a small child," said Rabie.

"There's photographs of it, Jim," Schoening said, although he actually did not have such evidence in hand. "How about a picture of you lying on the floor, nude, next to Julie?"

"If I saw a picture of that I would have to believe it occurred," Rabie said.

While Rabie was being interrogated, Detective Paul Johnson and Detective Loreli Thompson had been assigned to question Ray Risch. They drove out to the trailer on a dead-end street where he lived with his wife, Jodie. Risch was feeling ill that night; that day he had been painting a car in the shop where he worked, and the fumes always left him feeling like he had the flu. He was lying on the couch watching TV at ten-fifteen when he heard the squad car turn into the dark cul-de-sac. For the detectives, the fact that Risch was looking out the window as they approached the house seemed suspicious, as did his first remark when he answered the door: "Is this about Paul?" Risch immediately agreed to go to the station. He didn't think it was surprising that he would be questioned, even at this hour at night; but he did notice that when he went to get his jacket and shoes, one of the detectives followed him into the bedroom.

As they arrived at the Thurston County Sheriff's Office, Risch noticed Rabie's El Camino in the parking lot. A moment later, Risch was sitting in another interrogation room having his rights read to him. Until this point, he maintains, he still thought the detectives were interested only in Ingram. He never dreamed he was also a suspect.

"I noted that Risch's legs were crossed both at the knee and at the ankle," wrote Detective Thompson in her report. In her opinion, Risch's body language indicated that he was protecting something. "I also noted that when questioning would become intense at points, his arms would cross tightly across his chest."

On being confronted with what appeared to be overwhelming evidence against him, Risch offered the same sort of equivocal statements about memory that both Ingram and Rabie had. "I wasn't present that I know of, unless I blocked it out of my head," he said.

The interrogations went on into the early morning—Rabie in one room, Risch in another, and Peterson, the ubiquitous psychologist, shuttling back and forth. "We're talking about a situation here, Jim, where you have, if you will, a cult," Vukich told Rabie, offering what was becoming the official theory. "A cultist-type attraction and activity between these . . . individuals that has continued over a prolonged period of time."

Eventually each man was told that his friend had broken down and was implicating him, although this was not true. "This has gone far enough!" Risch cried.

"Paul said you guys bullied him and you made him do this and he didn't want to," Schoening told Rabie. "Ray is saying basically the same thing. Only, he's saying that he was the one who was the weakling, and he's saying you and Paul were the worst two."

Rabie realized that this could be a bluff, but he was also aware that in a case like this, which had multiple suspects, one person could be offered a certain degree of immunity to provide testimony against the others—and that often it was a scramble to pin the ringleader tag on another suspect. "Give me the responsibility, because I've blocked it out enough—I must be the worst one," Rabie said glumly. "The only option is to lock me up, and you're going to have to throw away the key, because if I can't remember this, then I am so damn dangerous I do not deserve to be loose."

5

The next day, December 2, Ingram met in Vukich and Schoening's office with Pastor Bratun. "I know I have a demon in me," Ingram said, and he asked Bratun to perform an exorcism.

"You don't have a demon, but you've got several spirits," Bratun told him. Bratun had spent some time in Southern California, where he had had some experience with people who were in bondage to spirits. He set a wastebasket in the middle of the floor and called out from Ingram the spirits of sexual immorality and gluttony, among others. As he did, Ingram attempted to regurgitate into the wastebasket, with little success. Still, he felt "delivered," he said, and when he went back into the interrogation room he produced a new memory. In this memory, Rabie, who is five feet eight inches tall, pushed Ingram, who is six feet two, down the stairs. "He wanted to do something that I didn't want him to do," Ingram told the detectives. "He said he wanted Chad." Rabie shoved his way into Chad's room. "Chad was on the bed and cowering. He went over and ripped his pants off and made him kneel on the floor and I was powerless to do anything. . . . He forced Chad down and had anal sex with him." Chad was thirteen or fourteen at the time. "When Jim was done, he got up, put his pants back on. He said he'd do that any time he wanted to,"

Ingram related. "He'd kill us if we said anything. He had control."

That afternoon, Detective Loreli Thompson interviewed Chad, then twenty years old. The young man said that he had never been abused, sexually or in any other physical manner, by his father or anyone else. "He said he had never really talked with Rabie beyond a casual hello," Thompson noted. Chad admitted that his father sometimes lost control and yelled at the children, but otherwise their relationship was "O.K." The young man was beginning to have doubts about the veracity of his own recollections, though. Recently, he and his mother had been looking through family photographs and other household items in an effort to prompt their memories. So far, neither of them was able to remember anything extraordinary.

Paul's memory, however, was becoming more and more active and intricately detailed, aided by the visualizations that Peterson and the detectives encouraged and by constant prayer and assurances from Pastor Bratun that God would not allow thoughts other than those which were true to come into his memory. Ingram began seeing people in robes kneeling around a fire. He thought he saw a corpse. There was a person on his left in a red robe who was wearing a helmet of cloth. "Maybe the Devil," he suggested. People were wailing. Ingram remembered standing on a platform and looking down into the fire. He had been given a large knife and was expected to sacrifice a live black cat. He cut out the beating heart and held it aloft on the tip of the knife. "At one point, Ingram said that the cat might have been a human doll," Schoening wrote in his report. "This was related by Ingram as a third party looking at the scenario, i.e., I see; I feel; reminds me of; I hear, etc." Ingram also produced a memory of himself and Jim Rabie murdering a prostitute in Seattle in 1983, thereby implicating both of them in an infamous unsolved murder spree known as the Green River killings. The bodies of at least forty women had been found in Washington and Oregon between 1982 and 1984, and the authorities believed it was the work of a serial killer. At Schoening's request, the Green River task force looked into Ingram's memories of the slaying but could find nothing that corresponded with any of the victims.

Where were all these memories coming from? Were they real or were they fantasies? If they were real, why couldn't any two people agree on them? The Ingram daughters had said nothing about satanic rituals, but through the church grapevine they were getting the gist of their father's latest revelations, which Pastor Bratun often knew about before the detectives heard them. Ericka confided to a friend that her father was talking too much and giving too many details—that he was saying things she didn't want to remember, and she wished he would just be quiet.

Ericka herself was now saying that her father had sexually abused her on almost every night of the last week she lived at home. Detective Thompson interviewed one of the deaf girls who had been living with the Ingrams (and had since moved to another foster home). The girl said that the Ingram house was full of hate. "I don't want—angry—ignore—don't talk with me anymore," she said through her interpreter. She remembered that Sandy and Ericka had bickered because Ericka wanted to leave, and that Ericka had been grounded. That was the most dramatic incident she could recall. She told Thompson that she had not observed any abuse.

On December 8, Chad went to see his father in jail. It was a shattering experience for him. Paul, who had always been so aloof from his children, was sobbing so hard that he could speak only in gasps. He managed to say that Chad had been a victim, and pleaded with him to try to remember the abuse. "You have to get it out," he cried.

"I've never seen him like that," Chad later told Schoening. "It's like it was a different person. It wasn't my dad there.

That wasn't my dad there. That wasn't my dad. . . . It didn't even feel like him when I hugged him."

Chad accompanied Schoening to the interview room, where Dr. Peterson was waiting. Before Peterson turned on the tape, Schoening advised Chad that he might be arrested because of Ericka's accusations against him, so from the beginning of this interrogation, which stretched over most of two days, there was an incentive for Chad to paint himself as a victim. He began, however, by once again denying that he had ever been molested. His main grievance in the family was that he had to do more chores than the other children. He did admit to attempting suicide three years before, when he was seventeen. "Probably something my dad said. I can't remember the specifics," he said. There was a pale trace of a razor cut on his wrist, or seemed to be. "Where is it?" Chad asked himself aloud, as he attempted to point it out to the detectives. "It's right here, right along the crease." The detectives did not indicate whether or not the scar was visible to them.

"It was something very traumatic to you that your dad said that really hurt you," Schoening said, theorizing. "Maybe it hurt your manhood."

Chad tentatively replied that his father might have called him a loser. "But I don't think he said that. I can't remember."

"You can remember what happened," Peterson admonished him. "You can choose to remember that if you want to."

"Like what?" said Chad, obviously confused. "What do you mean, 'remember'?"

"What he's sayin' is, it's there," said Schoening. "The memories are there. We're just tryin' to help you."

"I know, I know," said Chad. "They're there. I just can't—I just can't put the dot on it, though."

"Well, I'm not surprised," Peterson said. "It's not unusual with kids who've been through what you've been through to not be able to remember. Number one, they don't want to remember. Number two, they've been programmed not to remember."

"Mm-hm."

Some time later, Peterson said, "I can tell you that the way to being what you want to become—a healthy adult—is to deal with those memories."

"Mm-hm."

"Because they have—they—I say 'they' because I believe that there's a 'they' who have done this to you."

"Mm-hm."

At moments, the conversation lurched into therapy or instant psychoanalysis, as Chad was urged to reveal his thoughts about his family and his rather limited sexual experience. Eventually, the interrogators prodded the young man into talking about his mental problems. He admitted that he had heard voices inside his head. Then, in a painfully halting manner that reminded the detectives of his father's interminable pauses, Chad described vivid dreams he had had as a child: "People outside my window, looking in, but I knew that wasn't possible, because . . . we were on two floors and I would . . . I would have dreams of, uh, little people . . . short people coming and walking on me . . . walking on my bed . . . uh, I would look outside and . . . out of my door." The little people reminded him of the Seven Dwarfs, he said.

"Those are dreams of being invaded," Peterson declared.

"Yeah, and I would look out my door and I would see . . . a house of mirrors and . . . and no way of getting out."

"Of being violated, trapped in an inescapable situation," Peterson said, interpreting. "What happened to you was so horrible."

"Right."

"You want to believe it's dreams," Schoening said. "You don't want to believe it's real. It was real. It was real, Chad."

"No, this was outside my window, though," Chad protested, pointing out that his bedroom had been on the second floor. Also, his older brother had slept in the same room—why hadn't he ever seen anything?

"What you saw was real," Schoening insisted. "This same type of stuff has come out of your dad, too."

"Were you shaking in your boots or did you pee on the floor? Were you that scared?" asked Peterson.

"No, no," said Chad. He claimed he had no strong feelings about the dream, just a leaden sensation, as if he were stuck in concrete. "I couldn't talk. I couldn't move except to close the curtain," Chad went on. "The only thing I could feel was pressure on my chest."

"What was on your chest?" Peterson asked.

"Well, this is a different dream," Chad said, recalling a recurring nightmare of his adolescence. "Every time a train came by, a whistle would blow and a witch would come in my window. . . . I would wake up, but I couldn't move. It was like the blankets were tucked under and . . . I couldn't move my arms."

"You were being restrained?" Peterson asked.

"Right, and there was somebody on top of me."

"That's exactly real," Schoening said excitedly. "That's the key, Chad. That's what was really going on."

"Chad, these things happened to you," Peterson insisted. "They assaulted your ability to know what was real."

"O.K."

"Pretty hard to remember this?"

"No, it was like it was yesterday." Chad then recalled that when the train whistle blew, he would find himself on the floor, and a fat witch with long black hair and a black robe would be sitting on top of him.

"Look at her face," Schoening said. "Who is this person? Somebody who is a friend of your family's?"

"It was usually dark," said Chad. He said the witch's visits occurred once or twice a week, lasting for half an hour, until they moved out of the old house. "I would hear the whistle; I would feel the pressure on my chest; I would be on the floor; but I would never feel myself getting out of bed, moving to the floor, and then I would be on the floor and then I would be back in bed, but never feel myself going from the floor back to the bed." As for his brother, Chad recalled that when the witch was in the room, Paul Ross would be gone, "but then when I would wake up, I would look and he would be there."

"Who does this person remind you of?"

"I don't know."

"You don't want to know or you don't know?" Peterson asked.

"Probably I don't want to know."

"Somebody you respect?"

"Right."

"Is there something there physically to keep your mouth from making noise?" Schoening asked.

"No, because I remember breathing."

"What's in your mouth?"

"I don't know. A cloth, maybe."

"It's very important, Chad. What's it feel like in your mouth?"

"Uh, it's not hard."

"Just let the memory come," Peterson advised. "It's not what you think about, it's what you're trying *not* to think about." When Chad resisted being steered any further, Peterson and Schoening told him that he had been programmed not to remember anything. "Why'd you have to run away from it?" Peterson demanded.

And Schoening added, "You wanted to go somewhere safe, right?"

"No, it was safe here," said Chad. "I always felt safe."

"Even when all this was going on?" Schoening asked.

"Except for the dreams," Chad said, obviously bewildered. "I—Because I thought they were—I put them off as dreams."

"Destruction of his sense of reality," Peterson said authoritatively. "Destruction of any ability to feel. Total, absolute obedience and subservience to the group."

A few minutes later, Schoening said, "Let's go back to when you were fourteen to sixteen and this person's sitting on you." How much room did Chad think there had been between the witch's pelvic area and Chad's chin? Chad supposed there had been a foot or so. "They would sit there real high," Schoening reminded him. "And you got something in your mouth."

"Yeah."

"And it's not cloth."

"Right."

"It's not hard, like a piece of wood."

"Right."

"What is it?"

Chad thought a moment about this riddle and then began to laugh nervously. "You just made me think—oh, golly."

"What is it?" Schoening insisted.

"I don't know. I don't know."

"What were you thinkin'? C'mon."

"I thought it was a penis, O.K.? I—it could be."

"O.K., don't be embarrassed. It could be," Schoening said. "Let it out. It's O.K."

"I don't know what's happening to me," Chad said miserably.

Once the interrogators had been able to translate the nightmares into reality, the rest followed easily. The witch underwent a sex change, and Chad's initial certainty that he had never been abused was completely overturned. The little people of Chad's first dream, who had reminded him of the Seven Dwarfs, were reinterpreted as being members of a cult who regularly abused him over most of his life. But Chad had forgotten all of it, the interrogators told him. He had been conditioned to accept the abuse and then to repress the memories.

"By God, those who've done this to you ought to pay for what they've done," Peterson said. "And I'll tell you something—you have the right to sue those fuckers and get as much as you want from them."

"That'd be nice," Chad said.

"You're damn right it'd be nice. Pay for a college education."

"Yeah."

"Pay for a nice car. Get you started in life."

"Well, I've already got a nice car."

"Yeah, but do you have a BMW?"

When he came to the interview, Chad had been threatened with arrest. Now that he had accepted his status as victim, he was being offered a view of the rewards he might claim. Peterson urged him to "go public" with his new discovery. "Wouldn't it feel great to say this was real—it's not a dream?" said Peterson.

"That's why I want to see the faces, so I can . . . say these are the ones that did it to me," Chad concluded. "I have to put a face to it."

At this point the detectives turned off the tape.

Earlier, Chad had examined the same photo lineup that his sisters had seen, including some twenty driver's-license pictures, mostly of former employees of the sheriff's office. Of those pictured, Rabie and Risch had been the closest friends of Paul Ingram and the ones most likely to be recognized by the children. Chad knew both men well; in fact, he had done odd jobs for them on several occasions. But when he was first presented with the lineup, he couldn't identify any abusers. During the interval while the tape was off, Chad examined the pictures again.

"Who's the face in the dream?" asked Vukich, when the tape was turned back on.

"Jim Rabie," Chad answered.

The following day, Chad produced a memory of being assaulted by Ray Risch in the basement of the Ingrams' house when he was ten or twelve years old. At this point, Chad leaned forward and stared at the floor "in a trance-like state," Schoening's notes record. "Sometimes he would go for 5–10 minutes without saying anything and at one point, drool came out of his mouth and onto the floor."

6

Loreli Thompson has a playful manner, but she hides her eyes behind dark, silver-rimmed aviator glasses. As a young girl, growing up in Olympia, Thompson had been drawn to puzzles of every kind—codes, crosswords, mysteries—and by junior high she had decided she wanted to be a detective. When she finally achieved her goal, in November of 1984, she was the first female detective in the county. While she was still a rookie, she encountered her first pedophile, a man who had molested several young girls in an apartment complex. Thompson persuaded him to confess. She discovered that she had an instinct for sex crimes, one of the most puzzling departments of criminal behavior. In order to better understand the motivations of sexual offenders, Thompson got a master's degree in clinical psychology, which was added to her master's in criminal justice. Her reports are full of telling psychological observations.

She saw every kind of sexual offender, from sadistic rapists to exhibitionists and voyeurs. In many cases she found that an understanding pat on the hand would help lead the perpetrator to her ultimate goal, which was to persuade him to confess. Thompson tries to keep her cases out of the courtroom. It was often difficult for juries to make sense of sex crimes or sometimes even to believe that crimes had taken place, especially when there was little evidence other than an accusation. When the accusation came from a child, juries tended to be even more skeptical. Thompson had seen how easily confused children could become in the presence of a forceful defense attorney; moreover, most sexual offenses against very young children are digital or oral, which means that there is characteristically very little evidence, no sperm or scarring. In Washington State, there are three categories of what is still informally called statutory rape. First-degree rape or molestation of a child pertains to children under twelve and a perpetrator who is more than twenty-four months older than the victim—for example, an eleven-year-old girl who engages in sex with a fourteen-year-old boy. Second-degree rape involves children who are twelve and thirteen. Third-degree rape (the offense Paul Ingram was charged with, because these alleged offenses are ones that took place within the statute of limitations) occurs in the case of an underaged victim and a perpetrator who is more than four years older; a fifteen-year-old and a twenty-year-old cannot legally have sex in Washington, although two fifteen-year-olds can.

After Jim Rabie's retirement, Loreli Thompson came to be regarded as the best sex-crimes investigator in the county. Other departments would sometimes consult her, especially in crimes against children, and by the time the Ingram case came into her life, she had already seen perhaps three hundred child victims in Thurston County. Some were as young as two years old. Many had been repeatedly molested for years. Because of her reputation and skill, Thompson was given the delicate task of interviewing Julie. In her experience, there was nothing very unusual about two little girls growing up in a house with a pedophile. She witnessed the effects of child abuse every day. Paul Ingram's emerging satanic memories did sound a jarring note to Thompson, but then what else could explain the wreck of a girl who sat in her office, practically mute, idly shredding her clothing and pulling her hair? Julie was the most traumatized victim that Thompson had ever seen. She had more success in getting statements out of four-year-old children who had been raped and beaten. Julie would sometimes write about the abuse in her upright, legible script, but she simply could not speak about it aloud. Early on, Thompson came to believe that Julie had been tortured.

All the familiar road signs of a typical police investigation had been turned about. The detectives were groping to understand what was going on in their community—and, indeed, in their own department. The alleged central perpetrator was admitting to more depraved crimes than the victims were charging (until this point, neither of the Ingram daughters had said anything about satanic abuse). It seemed nearly impossible to coordinate all the accusations into a coherent set of charges. The investigators realized that they were probing into strange and unsettling territory. Jaded cops who regularly visited the worst precincts of the human psyche were thoroughly shaken by the emerging revelations of the Ingram case. The memories that Paul Ingram was producing were at once disjointed and intricately detailed, like shards of a shattered vase. Ingram could describe the ornate fragments, but he seemed to have no way of piecing them back together. Even more disquieting to the investigators was a growing conviction that the Ingram case was, as they frequently said to each other, "the tip of the iceberg"—the iceberg being the nationwide satanic conspiracy.

Brian Schoening took to sleeping with the lights on. The interviews with Ingram went on for hours and hours, sometimes from early morning until nearly seven at night. Schoening began to dread the daily gamut of emotions, which at night would be replayed in his mind as grisly nightmares. One scene in particular haunted him. It was based on the image of Julie being hogtied on the floor, although in Schoening's recurring dream the victim was his beloved granddaughter. He would try to reach her, but for some reason he never could.

In the dream, she always looked terrified, and she would call out her pet name for him, "Boppa." Sometimes the dream would come before Schoening could even get to sleep. He would often awaken crying or shouting out loud. In the morning he would return to a world where nothing was normal.

Any extensive police investigation is freighted with suggestive details that color the detectives' judgments about the suspects and the defendants. Thompson, for instance, interviewed the former wives of Rabie and Risch. Rabie's ex described him as insecure and claimed that in the latter part of their eleven-year marriage, which ended in 1977, he developed a taste for pornographic books and movies. He was never interested in the occult, however. He had a passion for Louis L'Amour westerns, and the only quirk in his personality that she could recall was his irrational fear of birds. The former Mrs. Risch said that her husband "walked out and left us on the first of June in 'seventy-six." She also alleged that Risch was a liar. What she meant by that, she said, was "it was difficult for Ray to face reality. He would take the situation such as in the area of jobs, he always had a fantastic prospect coming up and he was gonna get this great job—you know, lots of money. There were many times when he would tell me one thing and I would find out that it was not the truth. So I got to the point where I did not really trust his words on a lot of things." Risch never abused the children, the woman said, but her son once told her about a strange incident concerning Paul Ingram. "It sounded too fantastic, but now that this has come up . . ."

"What'd he say?" Thompson asked.

"He said something about one time when his dad had scared him, that he made him lay down in the driveway and Paul had driven the car over the top of him . . . and it scared him really bad. . . . This has got to be the imagin—" She suddenly broke off, then declared: "You know, no sane adult is going to frighten a little four- or five-year-old and make him lay down . . . but then again . . ." She didn't know what to make of it.

The psychologist, Richard Peterson, had never been involved in a police interrogation before, and he had no official role in this one beyond determining whether it was safe for the suspects to be at large. A former assistant professor of psychology at Oberlin College in Ohio, Peterson had come to Washington in 1982 to work for the Mentally Ill Offender program, which he did for two years before going into private practice in Tacoma, specializing in forensic and clinical psychology. Since that time, he had worked with as many as three thousand sexual offenders. He was a familiar presence in the jails and courtrooms of Washington State, where he was often called upon to testify about a suspect's mental condition. His active presence and that of Pastor Bratun at several key interviews would later become a subject of controversy in the defense of Rabie and Risch. At the time, however, the detectives were grateful for Peterson's participation. Peterson at least had some familiarity with these matters—the year before, he had had the unnerving experience of encountering patients who remembered being victims of satanic abuse.

Thousands of therapists have reported similar cases in recent years; but to Peterson, in 1987, it was still rare enough to be surprising. "Survivor" stories began to surface with the publication, in 1980, of a book called *Michelle Remembers*, written by a thirty-year-old Canadian named Michelle Smith and her psychiatrist, Lawrence Pazder (who later became her husband). The book describes Smith's memories of black-magic ceremonies and of atrocities she was subjected to by a satanic coven, which purportedly counted among its members Smith's mother. Smith recovered these memories while she was undergoing therapy, following a miscarriage. Usually the memories surfaced when Smith was in a hypnotic trance. Her account became a model for the many survivor stories that would follow, although, typically, there was no evidence that any of her story was true. Indeed, her sisters (unmentioned in the book) and her father deny that these fantastic events occurred, and police in her native Victoria, British Columbia, were unable to substantiate any of the baby sacrifices that Smith remembered. Smith's mother is deceased.

Most accusations of satanic-ritual abuse in the early eighties were attached to allegations of sexual molestation in day-care centers. In January 1988, Memphis's daily paper, the *Commercial Appeal*, published the results of an investigation into thirty-six such cases around the country. It was one of the first skeptical examinations of the ritual-abuse phenomenon. The reporters, Tom Charlier and Shirley Downing, found that most cases evolved out of a single incident involving one child; but through publicity and runaway police inquiries, the investigations spread, and subsequent accusations were made against police officers, defense lawyers, and even the social service workers investigating the complaints. In the thirty-six cases examined, ninety-one people were arrested and charged with abusing children or endangering them; and of the seventy-nine defendants whose cases had been settled, twenty-three had been convicted, most on lesser charges that had nothing to do with ritual abuse. There was virtually no evidence in any of these cases except for the uncorroborated stories of the very young children. Prosecutors in the day-care cases often used *Michelle Remembers* as a reference guide.

The best-known of these cases involved the Virginia McMartin Preschool, in Manhattan Beach, California, and it engendered the longest and most expensive ($15 million) criminal-court case in American history. Peggy McMartin Buckey and her son, Raymond Buckey, along with five other child-care workers, were charged with molesting 360 children over a ten-year period. It began in 1983 when a housewife, who had a history of mental illness, claimed that Raymond Buckey had sexually assaulted her son, who was two and a half at the time. She said that her child described airplane flights, animal sacrifice, and sex rituals inside churches. The Manhattan Beach Police Department then sent a letter to two hundred families whose children attended the preschool, saying that the police were investigating possible criminal acts, including oral sex, fondling of genitals, sodomy ("possibly committed under the pretense of 'taking the child's temperature' "), and the photographing of naked children. The panicked parents, who until then had not noticed any signs of abuse, were referred to the Children's Institute International. A nonprofit sex-abuse center, CII was run by a woman who interviewed children while wearing a clown outfit and who later testified before Congress that she believed in a network of "child predators" who were operating day-care centers as covers for child pornography. Soon children who initially had denied that any abuse had taken place remembered going to the cemetery on buses with shovels and pickaxes to dig up coffins. They told about teachers flying through the air and seeing naked nuns and priests frolicking in secret tunnels under the school (no such tunnels were ever found). Glenn E. Stevens, who was a co-prosecutor in the McMartin case, quit in disgust, denouncing the prosecution as a massive hoax. "If a child said no, nothing ever happened to them, the interviewer would then say, 'You're not being a very bright boy. Your friends have come in and told us they were touched. Don't you want to be as smart as them?' " Stevens said. Michelle Smith and other "survivors" met with some of the children and the parents in the McMartin case. Eventually, most of the charges were dropped and the others resulted in acquittal or mistrial; but by then there had been more than a hundred cases around the country in which children made accusations of fantastic abuse, usually involving details similar to those publicized in the McMartin case, such as devil worship, open graves, cannibalism, airplane trips, nude photography, being urinated or defecated on, and murdering babies. The McMartin parents formed a group called Believe the Children, which waged the campaign in the media and provided support for parents who felt that their children had been similarly abused. Within a year in the Los Angeles area alone, allegations of ritual abuse arose at sixty-three other day-care centers. One sensational case appeared in 1986 in Sequim, Washington, not far from Olympia, after a woman noticed a rash on her granddaughter's vagina. Five children later stated that they had been taken to graveyards and assaulted by adults in hooded robes. Charges against the preschool operator in Sequim and her son were later dropped because of insufficient evidence.

Peterson became sufficiently interested in the subject to conduct a survey of Tacoma and Seattle therapists in early 1988, and he found that a quarter of the respondents had treated victims of satanic-ritual abuse, or SRA, as it was coming to be known in the rapidly developing literature of the phenomenon. That same year, an influential paper appeared, under the title "A New Clinical Syndrome: Patients Reporting Ritual Abuse in Childhood by Satanic Cults." The authors were two psychiatrists, Walter C. Young and Bennett G. Braun, and a psychologist, Roberta G. Sachs, who specialized in dissociative disorders. These are psychiatric maladies characterized by an unintegrated sense of identity, the best-known of which is multiple-personality disorder, or MPD. People who suffer from dissociative disorders also have disturbances of memory, which can range from dreamlike recall to partial memory lapses—or fugue states—to complete psychogenic amnesia and out-of-body sensations. The authors interviewed thirty-seven people undergoing treatment for dissociative disorders who also spoke of having been victims of SRA. They found an astonishing similarity in the stories of the patients they analyzed. The most common abuses reported were of being forcibly drugged during rituals; of being sexually abused, often with sexual devices;

of witnessing the abuse or torture of other people or the mutilation of animals; of being buried alive in coffins; of being forced to participate in the sacrifice of human adults or babies; of being ceremonially "married" to Satan; of being impregnated during a ritual and later having to sacrifice the fetus or infant to Satan; and of being made to eat human body parts. It was a virtual checklist of the atrocities originally described in *Michelle Remembers*. "The lack of independent verification of the reports of cult abuse presented in this paper prevents a definitive statement that the ritual cult abuse is true," the authors conceded, but they went on to say: "Despite the fact that some patients have discussed ritual abuse with other patients, and the fact that patients have had contact with referring therapists who may have provided information to them, it was our opinion that the ritual abuse was real." Many other therapists, counselors, and psychiatrists were also coming to that conclusion. Furthermore, Braun saw a link between multiple-personality disorder and SRA; he believed that of the two hundred thousand Americans that he estimated were suffering from MPD, up to one-fourth could be victims of SRA.

Dr. George K. Ganaway, who is the program director of the Ridgeview Center for Dissociative Disorders in Smyrna, Georgia, observed the same link but drew a different conclusion from it. Ganaway suggested that dissociative disorders might account for the SRA phenomenon, rather than vice versa, because the alleged victims were highly hypnotizable, suggestible, and fantasy-prone. In a 1991 speech before the American Psychological Association called "Alternative Hypotheses Regarding Satanic Ritual Abuse Memories," Ganaway warned: "When individuals are highly hypnotizable, they may spontaneously enter autohypnotic trance states, particularly during stressful interview situations. . . . Experimental hypnosis evidence indicates that memories retrieved in a hypnotic trance state are likely to contain a combination of both fact *and* fantasy in a mixture that cannot be accurately determined without external corroboration." Furthermore, hypnosis increases the subject's confidence in the veracity of both correct and *incorrect* recalled material. Highly hypnotizable individuals suspend critical judgment while in trance states and compulsively seek to comply with the suggestions of the interviewer, Ganaway said. There was thus an obvious danger that an unwary therapist might unconsciously guide patients to conclusions that already existed in the therapist's mind. That concern had caused lawmakers in a number of states, including Washington, to reject testimony that had been enhanced through hypnosis. In an earlier paper, "Historical Versus Narrative Truth: Clarifying the Role of Exogenous Trauma in the Etiology of MPD and Its Variants," Ganaway had proposed that much of what was being remembered as satanic-ritual abuse was in fact an invented "screen memory" masking more prosaically brutal forms of actual abuse, such as beatings, rapes, deprivations, or incarcerations. This paper became a touchstone for mental health workers who believed that something awful had happened to their anguished patients but that, whatever it was, it was something other than satanic-ritual abuse.*

---

*Ganaway has since become more circumspect in asserting that real abuse occurred. "I was perhaps being charitable and even overprotective of colleagues who were claiming to be uncovering spontaneous, allegedly uncontaminated cult-related material," he wrote in 1992. "Whereas the screen memory hypothesis has proven to be a likely possibility in a small number of cases I have seen since then, regrettably the most common likely cause of cult-related memories may very well turn out to be a mutual deception between the patient and the therapist. . . . Once reinforced by the therapist, this belief system may become fixed and highly elaborated, sometimes with tragic consequences. In these cases the common denominator in the satanic ritual abuse phenomenon may very well turn out to be the therapists themselves." (Ganaway, "On the Nature of Memories: Response to 'A Reply to Ganaway,' " *Dissociation* 5, no. 2 [June 1992].)

A 1991 survey of members of the American Psychological Association found that 30 percent of the respondents had treated at least one client who claimed to have suffered from satanic-ritual abuse, and 93 percent of those who completed a second survey believed their clients' claims to be true. Another poll addressed the opinions of social workers in California. Nearly half of those interviewed accepted the idea that SRA involved a national conspiracy of multigenerational abusers and baby-killers and that many of these people were prominent in their communities and appeared to live completely exemplary lives. A majority of those polled believed that victims of such extreme abuse were likely to have repressed the memories of it and that (contrary to scientific evidence) hypnosis increased the likelihood of accurately recalling what had happened.

The question of whether SRA is real has riven the mental-health field. On the one hand, there are those who compare survivors of satanic-ritual abuse to people who claim to remember past lives or to have been abducted by aliens: the evidence—or lack of it—is about the same in each instance. On the other hand, there are those who compare survivors of SRA to the survivors of less spectacular forms of child abuse. They point out that in many cases memories of what one might call ordinary abuse are forgotten, and are recovered only in therapy, through exactly the same process that produces memories of ritual abuse. If some recovered memories are deemed authentic, they ask, then why not others? Where does one draw the line in deciding what to believe?

How delicate this argument has become was apparent at the August 1992 meeting of the American Psychological Association, in Washington, D.C. Michael Nash, an associate professor of psychology at the University of Tennessee, presented a clinical account of a patient who had reported remembering an abduction by aliens. "I successfully treated this highly hypnotizable man over a period of three months, using standard uncovering techniques and employing hypnosis on two occasions," reported Nash. He took the position that the abduction story was relevant therapeutic material but not literally true. "About two months into this therapy, his symptoms abated, he was sleeping normally again, his ruminations and flashbacks had resolved, he returned to his usual level of interpersonal engagement, and his productivity at work improved. What we did worked. Nevertheless, let me underscore this: he walked out of my office as utterly convinced that he had been abducted as when he walked in. As a matter of fact he thanked me for helping him 'fill in the gaps of my memory.' I suppose I need not tell you how unhappy I was about his particular choice of words." Nash went on: "Here we have a stark example of a tenaciously believed-in fantasy which is almost certainly not true, but which, nonetheless, has all the signs of a previously repressed traumatic memory. I work routinely with adult women who have been sexually abused, and I could discern no difference between this patient's clinical presentation around the trauma and that of my sexually abused patients. Worse yet, the patient seemed to get better as he was able to elaborate on the report of trauma and integrate it into his own view of the world."

The conclusion that Nash drew from this experience was that "in terms of clinical utility, it may not really matter whether the event actually happened or not. . . . In the end, we (as clinicians) cannot tell the difference between believed-in fantasy about the past and viable memory of the past. Indeed there may be no structural difference between the two." In reaction to Nash's speech, someone in the audience asked if he had ever considered another hypothesis in his treatment of the young man, which would explain everything: that the alien abduction had actually occurred.

Therapists were not the only source of information on SRA in 1988, a seminal year in the spread of the phenomenon. On

October 25, just before Julie wrote the second note to her teacher, disclosing the abuse by her father and the poker players, the Ingram family sat down together and watched a prime-time Geraldo Rivera special on NBC entitled "Devil Worship: Exposing Satan's Underground." It was one of the most widely watched documentaries in television history, although it was only one of many such shows. (The day before, the subject of Rivera's daily program had been "Satanic Breeders: Babies for Sacrifice." Daytime talk shows had become obsessed with satanic abuse since the McMartin case.) "No region in this country is beyond the reach of the Devil worshipers," Rivera said on location in Nebraska. "Even here in the heartland of America, stories of ritual abuse crop up. The children you're about to meet were born into it. They say their parents forced them to witness bloody rituals and even, they say, to participate in ritual murder." Then he showed a clip of a young girl who testified, "My dad was involved in a lot of it. He's, like, one of the main guys; he's a leader or something. He made us have sex with him and with other guys and with other people."

That year also saw the publication of several books that discussed SRA, including *The Courage to Heal: A Guide for Women Survivors of Child Sexual Abuse*, by Ellen Bass and Laura Davis. Although this book is only one of many "survivor" books, it is by far the most successful, having sold more than 750,000 copies. It is sometimes called "the bible of the incest-recovery movement," and in terms of its consequences, it would have to be considered one of the most significant publications of the century. Neither of the authors is a trained therapist; Ellen Bass is a poet, and Laura Davis is a short-story writer, and both lead workshops on recovery. They make a number of assertions that have become commonplace in such books, such as the notion that childhood abuse is frequently forgotten and can be recovered in therapy. Much of *The Courage to Heal* is in the form of survivors' stories, including that of

"Annette," who grew up in an upper-middle-class home in the Midwest. Annette's parents were active in their church and leaders in their community, but they were also secret satanists—along with other prominent members of the town. Before she was twelve, Annette was impregnated, then forced to watch as her babies were sacrificed. "I completely blocked out the abuse," she writes. "I couldn't believe my parents had done such heinous things to me. My family had been so proper and clean, they squeaked."

According to one of Julie Ingram's friends, who talked to Loreli Thompson, Julie read a book about incest and then lent it to the friend. The friend could not remember the title. Julie admitted that "she cried the whole time she read the book," the friend recalled. "I was thinkin': 'The whole entire time?' I mean, I can understand at the really, really sad parts. . . . Well, Julie's really sensitive and she really cares about those kind of things. I guess that's Julie for you."

Another influential book that appeared in 1988 was *Satan's Underground,* by a woman writing under the pseudonym Lauren Stratford, which purported to be a true account of the abuse and sexual slavery she endured as a child. *Satan's Underground* became a paperback best-seller, and it was widely read in fundamentalist Christian congregations. For many religious believers, stories of satanic-ritual abuse merely confirmed a worldview they already strongly held. Hal Lindsey and Johanna Michaelsen, two other very popular Christian authors, endorsed *Satan's Underground* and thereby added considerably to its credibility. "If there is one thing that cult satanists do well, it's cover their tracks in such a way as to thoroughly discredit witnesses who might seek to come against them," Michaelsen wrote in the foreword. She elaborated what has become the standard explanation for the lack of evidence in cult crimes: "Animals are indeed killed and buried, but are later dug up and disposed of elsewhere. The children are frequently given a stupefying drug before the rituals so that their senses and perceptions are easily manipulated in the dim candlelight of the ritual scene. The pornographic photographs taken of the children don't show up because they're carefully kept in vaults of private collectors." Stratford first began to recall memories of her abused childhood when she was hospitalized for an unspecified "life-threatening disorder." In order to deal with the physical pain, the author underwent "guided imagery," which is similar to hypnosis, with a therapist. In the process, she recovered horrifying memories of being pressed into pornography by her mother, becoming a child prostitute, and joining a satanic cult. In one vivid scene, she describes being placed in a barrel as the mutilated bodies of sacrificed babies were dropped on top of her. Eventually, however, the original publisher decided to withdraw *Satan's Underground* after a well-researched article in *Cornerstone*, a Christian magazine, attacked the book as a hoax, and portrayed the author as a deluded and unfortunate woman—as it happens, from a rigid, fundamentalist Christian family like the Ingrams, from Tacoma, just north of Olympia—who had a history of self-mutilation and of making sexual accusations that were never verified. (The book has since been reissued by another publisher, with few changes.)

It chanced that in the summer of 1988 Ericka Ingram had noticed a copy of *Satan's Underground* on the coffee table of a house where she was baby-sitting and had asked if she could borrow it. When she returned the book, she said that she had read it all the way through. Later she told police that she had read only a few chapters, then tossed the book into the backseat of her car, because the shock of recognition had been too great to bear.

Thus two communities that normally have little to do with each other—fundamentalist Christians and a particular set of mental health professionals—found common ground in the question dominating any consideration of satanic-ritual abuse: whether to believe it actually exists. In the absence of evidence that these stories or memories of satanic-ritual abuse were real, one could either reject them as absurd, withhold judgment until evidence appeared, or accept them on faith. The middle ground was rapidly shrinking as the proselytizers for both groups spread the word that SRA was real and anyone who doubted it either was "in denial" or was part of the satanic underground. (Interestingly, the rise in reports of SRA coincided with the collapse of international communism, suggesting that one external enemy was being replaced by another, closer to home. Bennett Braun made this connection explicit in a speech in 1988, describing the satanic conspiracy as "a national-international type organization that's got a structure somewhat similar to the communist cell structure, where it goes from . . . small groups, to local consuls [sic], regional consuls, district consuls, national consuls, and they have meetings at different times.")

The Los Angeles County Commission for Women formed a task force in 1988 to call attention to the purported rise in satanic-ritual abuse, thereby claiming SRA as a women's issue, ostensibly because women and children were the main victims of cult crimes. The commission issued a report that defined satanic-ritual abuse as "a brutal form of abuse of children, adolescents, and adults, consisting of physical, sexual, and psychological abuse, and involving the use of rituals," and continued:

> Ritual does not necessarily mean satanic. However, most survivors state that they were ritually abused as part of satanic worship for the purpose of indoctrinating them into satanic beliefs and practices.
>
> Ritual abuse is usually carried out by members of a cult. The purpose of the ritual elements of the abuse seems threefold: (1) rituals in some groups are part of a shared belief or

worship system into which the victim is being indoctrinated; (2) rituals are used to intimidate victims into silence; (3) ritual elements (e.g., devil worship, animal or human sacrifice) seem so unbelievable to those unfamiliar with these crimes that these elements detract from the credibility of the victims and make prosecution of the crimes very difficult.

The report goes on to say that the central feature of ritual abuse is mind control, which is achieved through the sophisticated use of brainwashing, drugs, and hypnosis: "The purpose of the mind control is to compel ritual abuse victims to keep the secret of their abuse, to conform to the beliefs and behaviors of the cult, and to become functioning members who serve the cult by carrying out the directives of its leaders without being detected within society at large."

Elizabeth S. Rose (the pseudonym of a free-lance writer who says she herself is an SRA survivor) wrote in a cover story for the January/February 1993 *Ms.*, "People would rather believe that survivors—particularly women survivors—are crazy. This keeps many survivors from coming forward." The cover line read, "BELIEVE IT! CULT RITUAL ABUSE EXISTS." The frequent reference to the need to believe in ritual abuse arises from the long-standing cultural resistance to the reality of child abuse, but it also points to the quasi-religious nature of the SRA campaign. At Safeplace, the rape-crisis center where Julie Ingram sought refuge after leaving home, counselors say that the disbelief that usually greets such charges parallels the incredulity that often greeted bona fide allegations of incest and sexual abuse only a few years ago. Nevertheless, the counselors have frequent internal debates about whether the increasing numbers of women who come to them talking about satanic-ritual abuse and human sacrifice are telling the truth. "Here's my dilemma," Tyra Lindquist, the administrative coordinator of the center, said. "We are already struggling against a tidal wave of disbelief—it's a tidal wave! Nobody wants to believe how bad it really is for women and children. Whoever walks in or calls us on the phone will tell us what she needs to survive this minute, this day. Our job is to help her survive through recovery. It's not our role to believe or disbelieve."

A fourth group to become concerned with the SRA phenomenon was the police detectives charged with looking into the crimes of the alleged cults. Joe Vukich recalls going to a homicide seminar in Portland, Oregon, where a detective from Boise, Idaho, gave a presentation on cult crimes. "Folks, I'm here to tell you this stuff is going on!" the detective said. Vukich turned to an officer sitting next to him and remarked, "Not in my department. I'd know about it." Soon dozens of police workshops around the country were discussing the phenomenon. Michelle Smith and Lawrence Pazder were often featured speakers, along with specialist "cult cops," who were likely to be fundamentalist Christians.

On the Ingram investigative team, only Neil McClanahan, who had come from a mainstream Protestant tradition but had converted to Catholicism, would describe himself as a devout Christian. All three of the detectives—Brian Schoening, Joe Vukich, and Loreli Thompson—were born and raised Catholic, although Schoening and Thompson were no longer practicing.

During the investigation Schoening and Vukich traveled to Canada to participate in an SRA workshop. They listened to speakers discuss teen satanism and role-playing games such as Dungeons and Dragons. They were given an overview of the history of satanism, from the "magic theater" of eighth-century Greece to its sway in Hitler's Third Reich. They were presented with the modern occult teachings of Anton LaVey, the author of *The Satanic Bible* and founder of the Church of Satan. They were instructed in such esoterica as cult holidays and the protocols of a black mass. They were shown magical symbols, runes, and glyphs. It was an amazing experience for the two detectives, but most shocking to them was the fact that they were greeted as experts on the subject. Before long, Schoening and Vukich and other Olympia detectives were besieged by calls from police officers around the country who were also engaged in investigating recovered memories of satanic-ritual abuse.

Early in the Ingram case, Undersheriff McClanahan telephoned Supervisory Special Agent Kenneth V. Lanning at the behavioral-sciences unit of the Federal Bureau of Investigation Academy in Quantico, Virginia. Lanning, the FBI's research expert on the sexual victimization of children, had been hearing stories of sexual abuse with occult overtones since 1983. At first he had tended to believe the stories; but as the number of alleged cases skyrocketed, he had grown skeptical. Soon hundreds of victims were accusing thousands of offenders. By the mid-eighties, the annual number of alleged satanic murders had reached the tens of thousands. As a result of information provided by a prison official in Utah, word circulated in the police workshops that satanic cults were sacrificing between fifty and sixty thousand people every year in the United States, although the annual national total of homicides averaged less than twenty-five thousand. Believers contend that no bodies are found because satanists often eat their victims and have access to sophisticated methods of disposal. It amazed Lanning that police officers, who regularly complained about inaccuracies in the media and often joked about tabloid-television accounts of "true" crimes, were susceptible to such material when it involved satanism. Yes, there were psychotic killers who heard the voice of Satan, just as there were psychotic killers who heard the voice of Jesus, but that didn't mean that they were members of an organized religious cult, Lanning argued. If satanic-ritual murder was defined simply as a killing that was committed by two or more people whose primary motive was to fulfill a prescribed satanic ritual, then Lanning could not find a single documented case of the phenomenon in the United States. He worried that many officers were allowing their personal religious beliefs to affect their judgment.

Lanning told McClanahan that after looking into hundreds of similar stories, he had come to the conclusion that they were merely a symptom of modern hysteria. McClanahan replied that the Ingram case was different: he had a perpetrator who was confessing to the crimes and implicating other members of the cult, and there was a likelihood that he would obtain other evidence, such as scars and photographs. "Well, you've got more than anybody else," Lanning conceded. When McClanahan hung up, it struck him that the Ingram case was much more important than anyone had realized—that it was the one case in America that could prove, finally, that satanic-ritual abuse was real.

7

"Questions to Ask God," Sandy Ingram wrote on a scratch pad next to a grocery list in December 1988. "Has my life been a lie—Have I hidden or suppressed things bad things that have happened in the past. . . . Have I been brainwashed, oppressed, depressed—controlled—without knowing it." What had once seemed to her a happy, normal life was no longer recognizable. Her husband and three of her five children were describing an existence she could hardly imagine. The police were still trying to find and interview Paul Ross, and how could she guess any longer what he might say? Her day-care license had been suspended, so she couldn't reopen her center even if she chose to. How was she going to support herself and the one child still at home, her nine-year-old son, Mark? "What I would like to do for a job," she wrote. "Chore work, go to school, pediatrick nurse, art teacher."

Two days after Paul's arrest, Sandy had gone to see him in jail. She sat facing a milky sheet of Plexiglas. Paul came into the room beyond, wearing orange coveralls and looking pale and thin. He picked up the phone on his side of the divider. She realized that they would never touch each other again. It was as if Paul were in some other, unreachable realm of reality. They talked in generalities about the case, awkwardly trying to keep the conversation alive. Paul reminded Sandy to get her driver's license renewed. Then he said that Pastor John Bratun had instructed him to make a confession to her that had nothing to do with his arrest: he told Sandy about the affair he had had, which had been over for thirteen years. Sandy was devastated. If she hadn't known about the affair, she found herself thinking, then what else might she not have known about?

The house on Fir Tree Road was so empty. During the day, Mark was in school, and for the first time in her life Sandy was alone: no day-care children, no husband coming home for lunch, no enormous loads of laundry to be done, no family dinners. There was so much silence and time. Sandy went to the mall and got her ears pierced.

That empty period was about to change, however. During the first couple of weeks in December, concerns arose on the part of the investigators about Sandy's role in the abuse. Both Ericka and Julie had initially denied that their mother was involved, but as the investigators and others repeatedly questioned how so many dreadful things could have been going on in the house without Sandy's knowledge, her daughters began making small disclosures.

Ericka told a friend about the poker games, when the men came into her room. Her mother would sit on the bed and watch, Ericka said.

"Your mother was a cheering section?" the friend asked.

"Well, she wouldn't do anything," Ericka explained. "She wouldn't say anything. She'd just watch."

"We're talking about your mother!" exclaimed her friend, who was a mother herself and simply couldn't imagine such a scene.

"It was strange," Ericka agreed.

The troubled friend reported the conversation to the police.

Detective Vukich interviewed another friend of Ericka's, who had heard a similar account. Sandy would come in before the men arrived and "get her ready," the woman told Vukich. "She said that her mother would be touching her vagina at times."

"Did she say if that was strictly for the purpose of getting her ready or her mother was, in fact, sexually abusing her?"

"She used the words 'sexually abused.' "

"And how recent was that?" Vukich asked.

"She said it happened two times in the month of September," the woman answered.

The woman also related that Ericka had wondered whether her parents had given her drugs that affected her memory. "She said sometimes she had a hard time remembering what happened, and then all of a sudden it'd come back to her, but she didn't realize why she couldn't remember in the first place."

Vukich and Thompson met with Ericka on December 8. She was cheerful and talkative, according to Thompson's notes, until they asked again about her mother's role; then she became withdrawn and communicated only with a few words or by shakes of the head. She recalled an evening, when she was nine or ten years old, on which her mother had entered her room, followed by her father, Rabie, and Risch. Rabie had stripped her and made her pose while he took photographs. Risch had held a gun. There had been many other photo sessions. Her mother had watched while this happened but had not participated.

Loreli Thompson left in the middle of the interview to meet with Ericka's younger sister. One of the discordant features of the investigation was that each girl's story tended to leave out the other, although they had been roommates for most of their lives. There were other discrepancies. Julie had never mentioned anything about Sandy's being involved, nor had she spoken about pornographic photographs taken by Rabie or Risch. Unlike Ericka, Julie had not been able to say the names of these two men; whenever either Julie or Detective

Thompson referred to them, Rabie was called Number Twelve and Risch Number Fourteen, which is the way they were identified in the photo lineup.

When Thompson asked Julie if her mother knew about the abuse, Julie responded, "I do. I think she does." Had Sandy ever been in the room when "bad things" happened? Julie replied, "I don't think so." Thompson then asked when the last time had been that Twelve or Fourteen had photographed her. Julie slumped in her chair, drew her knees up to her chest, and wrote on a piece of paper, "Six years old." Where? "My bedroom," she wrote. Where was Ericka while this was happening? Julie shrugged. Where was her mother? No response. Then Julie wrote that Twelve and Fourteen had put their hands all over her body and told her she was special. Was anybody else in the room? Thompson asked again. Finally, Julie wrote, "My mom." She began to shake. Thompson asked if her mother had said anything to her. "She told me to be a good girl and that no one was hurting me." Then Julie began sobbing. Thompson ended the interview.

That Sunday Julie went to church, and while she was praying at the altar her mother came and knelt beside her. The eyes of everyone in the church were on them. Sandy had not seen either of her daughters for a month, since this catastrophe in their family began to unfurl itself in such a frightfully public manner. This was the only way she could arrange to see Julie, so she leaned over and whispered that she loved her and that she would not have let anyone hurt her. She said that she did not know what had been going on. Julie got up and left without a word.

Sandy was sitting at home when police investigators arrived with a warrant to examine the Ingram house once again. The detectives advised Sandy of her rights and said that they were investigating her involvement in photographing and sexually touching Ericka. They were hoping that their search would uncover the photographs of sexual abuse. Richard Peterson came along for the ride. While the investigators combed through the bedrooms, Peterson poked around. He said he hadn't noticed any family pictures in the house, so Sandy took him to the hallway, where they kept framed photos on the wall. Some of the trim was missing from the doorways, he observed. That seemed odd, although Peterson didn't realize that the Ingrams had done much of the work on the house themselves, and it was still partly unfinished. Indeed, their way of living seemed foreign to him. Sandy's canning closet was full of vegetables and fruits from her garden. She was so proud to be able to provide for her family; she even entered her canning into competitions at the county fair. But to Peterson, the fruit jellies and pickled okra and tomato sauces were evidence that the Ingrams were on the edge of destitution. Otherwise, why couldn't they buy their food at the grocery store? They even slaughtered rabbits, although, as one of the detectives noted in his report, it wasn't Paul who did the butchering, it was Sandy. She enjoyed it, she said.

Sandy was knitting at the dining room table, trying to stay calm as the detectives turned her house upside down. Accusation hung in the air. One of the men remarked that either Sandy knew what was going on and ignored it, or else she must have participated.

"I haven't done either," Sandy said. "I didn't know anything."

The detective responded by saying that Sandy should have known through her sex life with Paul that he had been fooling around with the kids and other people. But in Sandy's opinion, there had never been anything forced or weird in her sex life. It was "very normal, very fun, very dear, and very satisfying." She was completely stunned when one of the detectives told her that Paul had been a homosexual for most of his life.

The search uncovered nothing incriminating, although several items were collected for evidence. There were four plastic boxes containing old datebooks; the letter Paul Ross had written to Sandy when he left home; and two books, *The Pleasure Bond* and *Devil's Gamble*. The detectives also took a broken lock from Julie's door. Julie had stated that she had installed the lock to keep her father from coming into her room and raping her. She said he had broken in anyway. At the time, however, Julie had told her mother that she had put a new doorknob on her door while she was baby-sitting, but she had installed it incorrectly and managed to get locked into her own room with the little children. Finally Chad had kicked the door open to rescue them. Sandy had been sympathetic. She remembered telling Julie, "It's all right, we'll fix it. If you need a new doorknob, Dad'll be happy to put it on." Now Paul was remembering that, indeed, he had been the one to break the lock in order to get to Julie. Sandy didn't know what to believe anymore.

"Who are you most afraid of, Rabie or Risch?" one of the detectives demanded.

"I'm not afraid of anybody," Sandy said boldly, although at that moment she was close to panic. The detectives finally left when Sandy decided to call a lawyer.

Everything in Sandy's life was flying to pieces. The marriage that she had once considered secure and happy had been publicly exposed as a sham. Now her own daughters were accusing her of sexual abuse. Could such things really have happened without her remembering them? Was there a "dark side" to Sandy, as there must have been to Paul?

What terrified Sandy most was the likelihood that she would lose Mark. Someone had called the state's Child Protective Services and said that Mark had to be taken away from Sandy before the same things happened to him. The police knew that the anonymous caller was Ericka; she had been demanding custody of Mark. Sandy was afraid that unless she admitted that abuse had taken place in her home, she would be declared to be "in denial" and therefore an unfit parent. When Sandy spoke to Paul about her dilemma, in early December, he said that maybe it was a good idea to surrender Mark. At that moment, Sandy stopped defending her husband. "The house is very cold—and my heart is broken over & over," she wrote on a scrap of paper. "Things will not ever be the same."

On December 16, Sandy went to see Pastor John Bratun in his office at the Church of Living Water. Bratun was a kind-looking man, forty-three years old, with a long face and a mustache; he reminded Sandy of Tennessee Ernie Ford. He had been in Olympia for a little over three years; before that, he had served as assistant pastor for several Foursquare churches in Southern California. From the night of Paul's arrest, when Bratun went with Pastor Ron Long to comfort Sandy at the house, and then visited Paul in his cell, Bratun had been intensely involved in the Ingram case. Another church member, Paula Davis, who was Ericka's advocate, was present at most of her interviews. Information passed freely among the police, the church, and the victims.

Sandy would later say that she had always felt she could trust Pastor John, as she called him; and so she felt stung when he told her now that she was "eighty percent evil." He reiterated the speech that she had heard from the detectives: either she had known what was going on in her house and ignored it, or she had participated in it. She was probably going to go to jail unless she made a confession. Sandy bridled at the threat. "That may work with some people, but it won't work with me," she said defiantly. Still, she left Bratun's office feeling hurt and confused and even more afraid.

She was now almost completely alone; even her church had turned against her, and she could sense the relentless mechanism of the investigation bearing down upon her, ready to snatch her youngest child out of her hands and to grind away the small core of dignity that was left her in this sensational scandal. When she got home, she bundled Mark into the car and fled, forgetting to turn off the television in her haste. In a way, she felt, the escape was exhilarating. She had never driven even the short distance to Tacoma on her own, and now she was driving all the way across the state, through a snowstorm, to take refuge with relatives. She had never driven in snow before.

Paul, meanwhile, had produced another memory, this one involving Sandy. "It was late 1975 or early 1976," he told Schoening and Vukich. "I was at home with Paul Jr. and Chad while Sandy had gone shopping with the girls. It was about seven or eight at night. It was dark out and Jim Rabie, Ray Risch, and [another man] came over to the house. . . . Knowing that Sandy was gone, they wanted to have sex with the boys. We all went up to the main floor of the house to the first bedroom on the right and the boys undressed. I don't remember if they undressed themselves or we undressed them, but they did get undressed. Ray had on work clothes—clean coveralls and work boots. He and Jim undressed. I don't remember what Jim had on. Ray knelt on the floor and Paul Jr. sat on the bottom bunk of the bunk bed and leaned over and orally stimulated Ray's penis. At the same time, Ray was fondling Paul Jr. Jim Rabie also undressed and had laid Chad on the floor on his stomach, so that he could have anal intercourse with him. . . . Chad would have been seven to eight and Paul would have been eleven to twelve. . . .

"At this time, Sandy came home. All of a sudden. I don't know if the dog barked or whatever, but she came home. . . . I think she was early. . . . She had on a coat and she was carrying a package or a sack and the girls were behind her and our little dachshund came in with them. She kinda said hi as she came up and then when she saw what was happening, uh,

I suppose she dropped the sack and, you know, got very angry. I don't recall the words that were said. I do recall that she was very upset and very angry. Jim Rabie grabbed her by the hair and very forceful, very angrily, almost vicious, said, 'You can't do anything to us. If you say anything, Paul will go to prison and your family will be embarrassed.' And then he told her, he said: 'I'll kill the kids.' " This was a side of Rabie that Ingram had never seen before. Until now Rabie had always seemed a very gentle person.

"How were the boys reacting while all this was going on?" asked Schoening.

"I don't recall," said Ingram. "I can kinda see the girls running when they saw what was happening, when they saw the viciousness with which Jim grabbed Sandy by the hair and started screaming at her. They ran into the living room and hid. I believe I was kind of outside the room when all this was going on, and I don't know what the boys did."

Rabie and Risch and the other man took Sandy downstairs, Ingram said. They stripped her and ripped up a sheet and tied her to the bed frame. "She was spread-eagle on the bed," said Ingram. "Jim Rabie raped her first, and I recall it was vicious—you know, he wasn't nice at all about it. And then Ray Risch raped her." Rabie again threatened to kill the children if Sandy told.

"After they left, I untied her and she put something over her and sat on the end of the bed," said Ingram. "She said, 'Why?' " Ingram had told her that he had gotten involved in a witchcraft ritual. "I signed a contract with them where I promised secrecy and said I wouldn't reveal anything about the group or what they did." It was hopeless to resist, he believed. The only way out of the cult was by death.

"My memory is becoming clearer as I go through all this," Ingram said at the end of the session. "It's getting clearer as more things come out."

As Paul was giving his statement to detectives, Sandy was writing in her diary. "It is now Dec. 17th—I am in Spokane. Brought Mark here in case I get arrested," she wrote. "So much has happened I don't know if I can say it all—Jesus you know me better than I know myself—You know if all this is true. You know the truth—Please Jesus answer my hearts cry. Help me to get in touch with the truth with reality. I am afraid Jesus. I am afraid. Sometimes I am numb—sometimes I am excited about a new future. . . . Where have my children gone, my precious babies that I love—Forgive me Forgive me for not seeing—Oh Lord I do not understand. Help me to understand. Help! I took off my wedding ring Dec. 16th in Ellenburg."

8

On December 18, Detectives Brian Schoening and Joe Vukich finally located Paul Ross, the eldest of the Ingram children. His flight from home had led him to Reno, Nevada, where he was working in a warehouse. They went by his apartment; he wasn't home. Schoening left a note on the door asking him to call them at the motel where they were staying. He called at eight-fifteen the next morning. There was a warrant outstanding for him in Thurston County for malicious mischief—he was accused of having battered someone's car with a baseball bat—and he wanted to know if that was why the officers had come. No, Schoening told him, there was a problem in his family. His father and two other men, whom Schoening didn't name, were in jail, and his sisters were in protective custody. The rest of his family was safe. Schoening didn't reveal what the charges were, but when Paul Ross met with the detectives several hours later he guessed that his father had been charged with a sexual offense.

There are no recordings of Schoening and Vukich's interview with Paul Ross, only notes made by Schoening and the boy's own statements later. The detectives found Paul Ross to be hostile, bitter, and evasive. "I'd like to shoot my dad," he admitted. "I've always hated him." He said he wasn't surprised that his father was in jail, because his father had physically abused him. Specifically, the young man recalled an incident several years before in which his father had thrown an axe at him. Ingram had been standing on a deck behind the house, and Paul Ross and Chad had been in the backyard, below him. Angry because the blade was dulled, their father had thrown the axe from the deck, and if Paul Ross hadn't moved it would have struck him. What was significant about this memory was that, unlike so many others the detectives had heard, two other people had remembered it, and remembered it more or less the same way. Chad had said that it was a roofing axe that the boys had lent to a neighbor. It had gotten dull, which upset their father. He wanted the boys to sharpen it. Paul's account was that he had only meant to toss the axe down to his sons and had been surprised when it landed right at the boys' feet. He had always felt bad about the incident, he said, and supposed that this was the reason his eldest child had left home. The axe story had the feel of a normal memory; it was practically the only one in the case.

As the one person in the family who had not been exposed to the church grapevine and who claimed not to have heard about his father's arrest until that morning, Paul Ross was the least contaminated source the detectives had encountered. As they spoke to him, however, a now familiar fixated expression came over his face. He sat in the detectives' motel room, staring out at the foothills of the Sierra Nevada, and his voice took on the monotonous quality of a trancelike state. Schoening was incredulous. It seemed as if everyone he talked to on this case fell into a trance. For him, these interviews were an emotional seesaw; whenever one of the Ingrams went robotic, Schoening would start chewing the furniture. What was driving him crazy was the absence of feeling. He was filling in the pain, the outrage, the humiliation, the horror, from his own emotional palette.

Because the interview with Paul Ross was not recorded,

one cannot know how much information the detectives fed to him, or what might have been suggested while the young man was entranced. Vukich asked what he remembered about sexual abuse from his childhood. Nothing came to mind at first. He did recall the poker parties, and he mentioned the names of several of the players, including Rabie and Risch; then he picked out their photographs and those of several others. He said that he hated Rabie. He called Risch "a gay guy." When the detectives asked him to explain, Paul Ross recalled an evening when he was ten or eleven years old. He heard "a muffled cry, a yelp, almost like somebody stepping on a dog's tail." He crept downstairs to investigate. The door to his parents' bedroom was open just a crack. Peeking in, he saw his mother tied to the bed, "spread eagle," with belts around her feet and what appeared to be stockings lashing her arms to the posts. "Jim Rabie was 'screwing' her," Schoening's report related, "and his dad had his 'dick' in her mouth." Ray Risch and another man were "to the left, 'jacking each other off.' His dad came over and hit him so hard it almost knocked him out, yelled at him to leave them alone, and closed the door." Paul Ross then got a fifth of whiskey and retreated to his room. He became an alcoholic that very night, he said.

This story was so close to the memory that Paul had produced only a few days before. The detail about Sandy being tied to the bed was a match, almost like the axe story. And yet, if Sandy was a victim of such a brutal rape, why couldn't she remember it? Why couldn't Paul Ross remember his own abuse by Rabie and Risch the same night they raped his mother? What about the years of abuse his sisters endured—why didn't he know about or remember that? He did mention one occasion when his father came into the bedroom he shared with Chad and took his younger brother out of the room in the middle of the night. The boy was crying. That was all that came to mind.

In fact, there wasn't a single bit of Paul Ross's statement that the detectives could use. It was so tantalizing, so frustrating. They couldn't charge suspects for crimes the victims couldn't recall. If only Paul Ross could remember more, or admit that he also had been abused! As it was, Paul Ross was more of a liability than an asset to the prosecution. At one point, Schoening became so upset he backed the young man against a wall. "We know you're a victim!" he insisted. The young man demanded a break. He said he needed to be alone. He promised that he would be back in thirty minutes. He walked out and didn't come back.

He did locate his mother, however, and telephoned her for the first time in two years. "Mom, I know everything that happened," he told her, according to Sandy's later statement. She said he related what he had said to the detectives, including the rape scene. Sandy asked Paul Ross if he had repressed these memories and then suddenly recovered them. No, her son told her, he had always remembered them, but lately he had been going to a hypnotist who was helping him remember even more.

Sandy recalled the remark that Ericka's friend Paula Davis had made to her that night at Denny's when Ericka had first disclosed the abuse to her. "You're the only one in the family who didn't know," Davis had said. That must have been true, Sandy realized. Now the only person in her family, except herself, who maintained that he had never been abused was nine-year-old Mark.

On December 20, back in Olympia, Joe Vukich and Loreli Thompson met with Ericka and her advocate, Paula Davis, at the sheriff's office. Davis, twenty-nine, was a schoolteacher who described herself as Ericka's best friend. Under Washington state law, victims of violent or sexual crimes are entitled to have a spokesperson present at any interview. Given the victim's state of mind, the investigators thought it appropriate to conduct the session in a special room that had been set up—ironically, by Jim Rabie—for interviews with abused children. Ericka and Paula sat in miniature chairs, amid the plastic toys and security blankets.

Vukich asked Ericka if her brothers or her sister had ever discussed their abuse with her. "No." Ericka was monosyllabic. Sometimes it seemed that she didn't even hear the questions. Vukich managed to get her to say that the last time Rabie had molested her was three months earlier, in September.

"Was your sister in the room with you?" asked Vukich.

"No."

After a while, she whispered that she needed to stop for a moment. The detectives left her in the room with Paula. When Vukich glanced in through a small window in the door, he saw the two women sitting on the floor. Ericka was cuddled up in Paula's lap, sobbing. His heart went out to her. He'd never seen a grown woman reduced to such a state.

"Do you remember what we asked you, Ericka, about what Mr. Rabie did when he came over to the bed?" Vukich said when the interview resumed.

Ericka sat mute, shifting in her chair and tugging at a thread on her jeans. A minute passed.

"And this was the last week of September," Thompson said to break the silence.

"What was it that he did, Ericka?" Vukich asked again. "Did he make you do something to him?"

"Yes." She hid her face in Paula's shoulder.

"Did he make you touch him somewhere? You're shaking your head. Is that yes or no?"

"Yes."

"What part of his body did you have to touch, Ericka?" Thompson asked.

"Can we stop for a minute? I have to go to the bathroom," Ericka suddenly announced, and she left the room.

The detectives could hear her retching in the toilet. Davis went after her. The two women were gone for some time. When they came back, Ericka handed the detectives a sheet of paper on which she had written a detailed statement. Vukich read it aloud for the record:

> I was asleep in my room in bed and heard Jim Rabie come in and that's when I looked up and saw him. He started touching me with his hands first on the outside of my sweats, then underneath. He touched my chest and on my private parts, front and back. He inserted his fingers in my front and back private parts. He kept telling me to be quiet in a threatening voice. My mom and dad were awake someplace in the house. He forced my head to his front private part with his hands. He was very rough and hurt me with his hands. It seemed that this continued for a long time. I was scared and didn't know what to do. He had previously threatened me that he would kill me and do worse things to me if I refused or if I told. He thrust his front private part into my mouth repeatedly for a long time. Then he ejaculated in my mouth. His pants were down, but not off. Then he started making grunting noises. Then he started touching me orally with his mouth on my chest and front and back private parts. This seemed to continue for a long time and he was very rough and hurt me. Then he stopped and said I knew what would happen if I told. Then he urinated all over my body in bed. He didn't defecate on me this time. Later, my father came in.

Vukich could barely control his emotions as he read this; he felt overwhelmed by the monstrousness of the scene Ericka had just described. "I think I'd like to start at the end, where you say 'He didn't defecate on me this time,' " Vukich said gently. "Were there other times when this same scenario happened where he did defecate on you?"

"Yes."

When Ericka left the interview room, Vukich took her handwritten statement down the hall and threw it on his lieutenant's desk. "The son of a bitch shit on her!" he cried. His voice was quaking. He had never felt this way about a victim before. His feelings were more those of a protective older brother, he believed, or the loving father she had apparently never had—even though he was not that much older than Ericka. When the other detectives observed how emotional Vukich became in speaking about her, they joked nervously that he was falling in love.

The same day that Ericka was making this statement, Sandy drove back to Olympia. She had decided to leave Mark in the care of her relatives in Spokane in order to keep him out of the grasp of the Child Protective Services. She knew, however, that she wouldn't be able to hide him forever.

Sandy went straight to Pastor Bratun's office. This time, Bratun was more understanding. He explained to her that when he had said she was eighty percent evil he was also saying there was a side to her that was twenty percent good. This was the side that had brought her back. This was the side that was trying to remember. To encourage her he revealed some of the new memories that Ingram was producing. Many of them concerned satanic scenes. One involved a former girlfriend of Ray Risch's, who Paul said was the high priestess of the cult. Paul had remembered having sex with her after a ritual in a barn. He had signed an oath in blood, pledging loyalty to the cult. If he tried to break away, his younger daughter would be killed. Sandy said she couldn't remember any such scenes. Paul had also recalled Sandy having sex with Risch, Bratun told her. He asked if that had ever happened. Sandy said no, then hesitated. "Oh, no!" she cried, and fell forward, burying her head between her knees.

The first memory Sandy produced resembled the scene her

eldest child had described. She was not tied to the bed, however, and it was Risch having sex with her, not Rabie. Paul stood to one side, guarding the door. Then another memory surfaced. This time she was tied up, but she was on the living room floor. Rabie was there, naked, and for some reason he was on all fours, howling like a dog. Sandy then saw herself in a closet with Paul. He had hold of her hair and was hitting her with a stick of kindling. The others were in the living room, laughing at her, calling her fat. Paul pulled her out of the closet and hurled her on the bed, where Rabie and Risch had anal intercourse with her. It seemed to Sandy that these events must have happened sometime before 1978.

After leaving Bratun's office, Sandy returned to Spokane to spend Christmas with Mark.

Paul Ingram had just been transferred to a jail in another county. His bail was set at $200,000. Once he was away from the daily interrogations and the constant reinforcement of the detectives and the urgings of his pastor, he began to have renewed doubts about the accuracy of some of his memories. A Christian counselor hired by Ingram's attorney administered a series of diagnostic tests. On the Minnesota Multiphasic Personality Inventory (MMPI), Ingram showed himself to be adaptable, resourceful, and self-reliant, if also restless, nonconforming, and easily bored. "Individuals who have this MMPI profile often perceive the world in different and original ways," wrote the counselor in his report. "They may be perceived as somewhat eccentric, unpredictable, or imaginative. They tend to think differently, at times negatively, and frequently are perceived as aloof, touchy, emotionally distant or apart, and preoccupied." The Millon Clinical Multiaxial Inventory (MCMI) revealed a person with an exaggerated need to be liked. Ingram showed a "rigid and tense compliance to social convention." He was the kind of person who was prone to follow orders. People such as Ingram "tend to show a perfectionist element, and condemnation causes them considerable tension, especially if conveyed by persons in authority. . . . This overall cooperativeness may hide strong rebellious feelings that may occasionally break through the front of propriety and restraint. These individuals lack insight, are often indecisive, and are easily upset by deviations from their daily routine. A pattern of rigid self-control is typical, and individuals with this profile only occasionally relax the edgy tension and guarded defensiveness that conceal their anxious feelings." The Rorschach test described a person who "has difficulty getting the whole picture." In the opinion of the counselor, Ingram "distorts data to meet his own needs rather than showing an outright thought disorder."

Ingram insisted on taking the Sexual Addiction Screening Test three times—once giving answers based on his state of mind before his arrest, once for the period before Pastor Bratun came and delivered him of demon spirits, and once for his current state. The first exam showed him to have no sexual deviations at all; however, on the basis of Ingram's responses in the two other exams, the counselor diagnosed him as a pedophile and a "walking time bomb."

The counselor also talked to Dr. Peterson and Pastor Bratun about Ingram. Peterson described Ingram as highly manipulative and completely separated ("dissociated") from his feelings, so much so that Peterson believed that Ingram had two ego states—a split personality, in layman's terms. He also recognized the effects of cult programming on Ingram. Bratun agreed with Peterson's observations. He saw the two ego states consisting of, on the one hand, a hardworking, civic-minded, loving father, who was so priggish he "wouldn't let his daughter come downstairs in a nightgown," and, on the other hand, an angry, violent, and manipulative individual who was the polar opposite in every respect of the Paul Ingram most people knew and respected. In Bratun's opinion, the exorcism in the jail cell had been the key moment in integrating these two opposing halves.

"He speaks with very flat responses, and no affect," the counselor reported. "It appears that he gives himself permission to 'get a memory' when this is done in a Christian context. Mr. Ingram appears to be a product of a dissociative disorder in which there is more than one personality that is capable of assuming control. He does not, however, appear to fit the criteria of multiple-personality disorder. Mr. Ingram does appear to have been affected by periods of intense indoctrination around cult issues. . . . In a sense, the longer his secret life remained separated, and the more pressure was brought by external forces to do more and more deviant sexual acting out, the more tightly he bound the walls of his separate, dissociative life." The Christian counselor added that, as Ingram was prayed for, "he began to make the tightly bound compartments mentioned above (separate ego states) porous and allowed some of the memories to begin to return." This defense counselor would eventually testify for the prosecution.

It was a stark Christmas for many families. The detectives found that the Ingram case was following them home, when they had the chance to be home at all. They certainly weren't in a holiday mood. To cheer them up, Ericka brought in a plate of Christmas cookies. Undersheriff McClanahan was so worried about the mental health of his investigative team that he assembled a team of psychologists to debrief them. The detectives were encouraged to express their feelings candidly, but they reacted so furiously that the psychologists beat a retreat and diagnosed the whole bunch as suffering from post-traumatic stress disorder.

Rabie and Risch were both in solitary confinement. Rabie was still pleading for a lie detector test. He refused to take his medication for narcolepsy and spent much of his time sleeping; it was the only time he had ever felt grateful for his affliction. During his waking moments, the former detective pored obsessively over the police reports of his case, which his attorney had secured. Risch lost forty pounds in solitary, and his hair, which had been jet black, turned completely white. His wife worried that he might have suffered a stroke; one day, he suddenly seemed unable to complete a sentence. His thoughts wandered, and he had difficulty hearing.

On the day after Christmas, Sandy returned, again alone, to the house on Fir Tree Road. "Dear Paul," she wrote that day, "I am praying for you that you can be totally and wholly restored. . . . Sometimes I am very afraid. Afraid because of what has happened in the past. . . . Sometimes I am even afraid of you Paul mostly because I do not know the truth. Was I controlled by you." Apparently contradicting what she told Pastor Bratun, she continued, "I am not remembering anything, but with God's help I will remember. I was very tired after driving today. I was also very upset—and didn't want to come back here. I didn't want to leave Mark." Then she began to draw upon other memories, memories that she and Paul shared. "Do you remember Paul Ross he was such a good baby so smart—do remember Ericka so beautiful, so tiny a diaper just wouldn't fit. And Andrea—How they would cry every night and I would sit & cry & hold them and as soon as you come home & took one of them they would quit crying—& Chad how badly you wanted another boy—He was a delight a quite delight always telling funny things He was hard to correct because everything he said would make you laugh—" Here the handwriting became skewed, and it spilled over the ruled lines of the stationery. "Paul, Do you remember how we meet—How shy you where? Do you rember that first drive in movie I remember but not the movie Do you rembere even before we married how we said or you said if we were unfaithful that was it Do you Remember—all the Ice Cream—when I was pregnant with Paul Ross—"

The last line ran off the bottom of the page.

9

On December 30, Ericka and Paula Davis returned for another interview session with Joe Vukich. Ericka wrote out a new statement:

Mom

She used to spank me at first when I came home from kindergarten. That was for doing nothing wrong. She would spank me very hard for a long time. Later she would spank me with wooden things or whatever she could get in her hands brushes things like that. Most of the time she was angry and would hit or kick or push. She never defended me or the other kids when our dad would come beat us. They had polls [poles] and she would use them as sexual devices to hurt me. The polls were like things used in a closet for hanging things on, made out of wood. She would do that when my father was also not there. Other people also saw these polls. She just told me not to talk about things that were happening or say I don't want to ever hear you say that again. From the time I was about 5 yrs old until the time I was about 12 yrs old. until we moved from 89th St. I remember being carried from my bed, by my father in the middle of the night. There were many people there waiting outside by the barn. Some of them were Jim Rabie, Ray Risch, Mom, Dad, High Priestess in a robe the people wore white, red & black.

There were many men there & some women. They chanted as I was carried out. It was cold out middle of the night and all I wore was a nightgown. My mother walked with us to the barn from the time I was taken from my bed until the time I we were in the barn. There was a table inside the barn. There was also a fire. All the people around the table including my mom & dad wore a gown & a hat resembling a viking hat with horns. There was a lot of blood everywhere. There was pitchforks in the ground—that was also used to threaten us with. The sacrifice. They would lay it first on the table then the high priestess would pick it up all the people would chant & the women would say words then the baby would be put on the table & all of the people including my mother & father circling the table would stab it with knives until it died. They continued to do this for a long time sometimes even after it was dead. Then they would all walk to the pit and chant and the high priestess would carry the baby and put the baby in something white then put it in the ground. Then they would bury it. The baby was a human baby about 6–8 months old. Sometimes they would use aborted babies. They would tell me this is what would happen to me also. They also would say you will not remember this. They would say it over & over again like a chant.

It was the first time that anyone in the Ingram family other than Paul had mentioned satanic rituals. His accounts had not included any mention of human sacrifice, however. Ericka then drew maps of the old house and the new one on Fir Tree Road, indicating where the ceremonies were held and where the babies were buried.

Loreli Thompson was beginning to get suspicious of some of Ericka's stories, which seemed to change with every telling. In the morning briefings she urged Vukich to be more confrontational. There were some other details that didn't add up, she insisted. Why did the daughters have to tell their mother about the abuse if, in fact, she was involved? Vukich was defensive; he believed Ericka was still too traumatized to respond to such close questioning. The truth was that all the detectives were turning into advocates for the victims they had been assigned. Schoening had become very protective of Sandy, just as Thompson had with her charge, Julie. Thompson worried that if she pushed too hard Julie might hurt herself. It wouldn't be easy to live with a suicide on her hands. But Thompson realized that if Julie was ever going to be able to testify, she would have to respond to the contradictions in her story. The next time Thompson met with Julie, she asked specifically why Sandy would have inquired about the abuse that morning in November, when she picked Julie up at school just before going on vacation with Paul. Julie wrote down, "I think she ask me to make it look like she didn't know." Julie looked exhausted; she said she had not slept well in days. Thompson asked Julie if she had been in communication with her sister about the case. "She called me and told me about satanic stuff," Julie acknowledged. Did she remember anything like that? "I remember burying animals," she said. "Goats, cows, and chickens." Were these natural deaths? Julie didn't know. Did she ever go to parties where people were wearing costumes? Julie became thoughtful. "No," she finally answered. Any ceremonies besides church? She shook her head no.

When Thompson inquired about an abortion Julie said she had undergone, Julie wrote, "I was 15 year old. I remember driving for about 30–45 min. and the doctor office was very little and an orange color. The only thing I remember about the abortion was pain. I screamed it hurt so bad." Her father had taken her to the clinic. That was about all she could remember.

"I then asked if there were marks or cuts on her body from the abuse," Thompson wrote in her report. "She shook her head yes, radically. She showed me her forearms. I noted two

light cuts on the right arm and two round marks on the left arm. These were small round marks similar to a burn mark. All of the injuries were on the forearms. I inquired about cuts on her upper arms, back and legs. She wrote down, 'Yes,' that there were injuries there. I asked how these wounds were inflicted. She wrote down, 'With knives.' . . . I asked who did this to her. She wrote down, 'Jim Rabie and my dad.' "
Julie then put her head down on the table and began to cry. Thompson asked if she might let her see the scars, but Julie adamantly refused.

The sisters' inability to actually talk about their abuse was becoming a problem as the trial date of Rabie and Risch approached. Rabie was charged with seven counts of statutory rape in the second degree, rape in the second degree, and indecent liberties. The charges against Risch were three counts of statutory rape in the second degree and rape in the second degree. Gary Tabor, the chief prosecutor, met with Julie in Detective Thompson's presence. A conservative, deeply religious man who still speaks in the flat, nasal tones of his native Oklahoma, Tabor has a heavy-lidded gaze, a gap-toothed smile, and a reputation as the smartest prosecutor in the county. Even he was confounded by all the rabbit holes in the Ingram case, however. From the prosecution's point of view, this recent note of satanic-ritual abuse was more than troubling, because juries tend to disbelieve such allegations. Tabor longed to keep the case simple, but it went on metastasizing and invading new territory. He could easily imagine what a clever defense attorney might do with the mass of contradictory memories that constituted the case against Rabie and Risch so far. Moreover, the victims appeared to be so traumatized that it was an open question whether they could testify in court. Tabor was trying to size up Julie as a witness. What he saw was not encouraging. She could not make eye contact. She pulled chewing gum out of her mouth in long strands. Tabor asked her if she was having trouble remembering the abuse. Julie replied that she just remembered things as she went along. She began tearing at the rubber sole of her shoe. Tabor asked how her mother had acted when she came into the room before the men came to abuse her. Julie didn't answer. Tabor and Thompson then watched as Julie peeled the sole off her shoe.

In a letter dated January 18, 1989, Sandy wrote:

> Dear Ericka and Julie,
> Mark is doing fine. . . . I call him everynight and see him every week. . . .
> Also I do have the house & 4 acres on the market to sale for 79,500 I still owe the bank about 48,000. Also have the other 6 acres for sale in two acres pieces. As soon as anything sales, I will be putting money into your savings accounts. I am hoping I can give each of you—Chad & Mark & Paul Ross also—enough money so that you can relocate, or go to college or do whatever you desire. . . .
> I am also planning to go to college and to relocate. Also I will be taking back my maiden name & start again.
> I am not talking with Paul because as I remember what has happened to me I am very much afaird. . . .
> If there is anything that you think you want from the house please let me know. Ericka I thought you might like your dishes from Greece. . . . I can put some things out like that & we can make arrangement for you to come & get them.
> I am paying your medical bills & your insurance & car payment & will continue to do so for a time—but I have no income until something sells. . . .
> Again I ask for your forgiveness. I trully did not know what was happening and I am just beginning to remember what did happen to me & I have remember something that have happened to you both. I do not understand it all or

remember it all yet. But I will and they are not above the law and you both do not have to fear any longer. . . .

Love Mom

The day after Sandy wrote to her daughters, Loreli Thompson drove Julie to Seattle. Both sisters had spoken of having had abortions, in addition to severe scarring from other abuse. The attorneys for Rabie and Risch had been pressuring the court to have them submit to a physical examination to verify that the abortions and scarring were authentic. Julie had finally agreed to see a female doctor who specialized in treating abuse victims. All the way to Seattle, Julie was quiet. Thompson knew how much she hated talking about the case, so it wasn't surprising that she'd be solemn. When they arrived, Julie insisted on going into the examining room alone.

Earlier, Julie had told Thompson that the scars on her body made her so self-conscious that she never changed clothes in the high-school locker room and never wore a bathing suit without a T-shirt to cover her. When Julie emerged, the doctor told Thompson that there was no lingering evidence of an abortion, but that its absence wasn't conclusive; often there would be no residual scarring, particularly in a very young woman. Repeated vaginal or anal abuse would not necessarily leave a mark, either; so the fact that the doctor found none was not unusual. The epidermis, however, is less forgiving—it would tend to reveal physical abuse. But the doctor had found no marks or scars anywhere on Julie's body.

Julie was unusually chatty on the ride back to Olympia. This time, it was Thompson who was quiet. There should have been scars, she kept thinking. Julie had said there were scars.

Later, the same doctor examined Ericka; except for mild acne her only scar was from an appendectomy.

"Would it be possible for someone to be cut superficially and for that to heal without making a scar?" Thompson asked.

"I would think any significant cut would probably leave a scar," the doctor said.

As for evidence of Ericka's abortion, the doctor told Thompson that Ericka denied that she had ever been pregnant; in fact, she claimed that she had never been sexually active.

In every successful investigation, there is a point of coherence, where the mass of assembled facts takes on a pattern. The detectives can begin to draw inferences; they can recognize the probable truth and the probable lies. The Ingram case was moving in the opposite direction: what had seemed to make sense in the beginning was becoming ever more mysterious; the mass of facts grew enormous, but the patterns kept dissolving. Compounding the puzzlement and the general sense of panic was the fact that the case against Rabie and Risch was moving steadily toward trial, like a barrel approaching a waterfall.

Joe Vukich saw Ericka again on January 23. Ericka had new disclosures to make, and once again they were so painful that she had to make them in writing. She described being abused by her mother, her father, Rabie, and Risch with leather belts and various sexual toys and bondage devices while someone took photographs. Sometimes she was gagged or whipped. She remembered a thick wooden paddle with holes in it. She was threatened with guns and knives. When Vukich asked about her abortion, all Ericka would write was, "It was at night." He tried to press her to say more, but she indicated it was too hard to talk about. Then Paula Davis wrote this statement for her:

> My father made me perform sexual acts with animals including goats & dogs. My father made me fondle their genitals first. Sometimes I was on my hands & knees & sometimes I was lying down. He would bring the animals to me & have

them perform oral licking to my genitals. Sometimes I was on my period, sometimes not on my period. Then my father would force me to have vaginal intercourse with the animals, While he took photographs. My mother was also present & also had intercourse with the animals.

These events had taken place from the time Ericka was in kindergarten until she was in high school. While Davis took down the statement, Ericka doodled on another sheet of paper—little flowers and what appeared to be a frowning butterfly.

10

The trial date for Jim Rabie and Ray Risch had been set for February 1989, just a couple of weeks away. Although they had made statements that the investigators found equivocal, both men maintained their innocence. As the prosecution prepared its case, Gary Tabor continued to have doubts about whether Ericka and Julie could testify. Only recently had Sandy come forward to make statements implicating the defendants, but these had concerned her, not her daughters. The statement of Paul Ross might do more harm than good to the prosecution's case, since he was unable to verify the abuse to his sisters. Schoening and Vukich went back to Reno to try to talk to the eldest Ingram child again. After nearly two hours of pleading, the detectives thought they had persuaded him to give them another statement, but the young man didn't show up the next morning as promised. The detectives went to his apartment several times and left notes on his door. No one appeared to be home. The next day they went again. This time they heard the stereo playing inside the apartment and the sound of laughing. They knocked and called through the door, but no one would answer. Finally, they flew back to Washington State—only to find that Chad had begun to recant. He was now declaring that the entire scenario he had given to investigators was only a bad dream.

That left Paul Ingram as the sole reliable witness in the case. He had pleaded not guilty in his first court hearing, in December, but Tabor saw that as a routine plea. Ingram had always indicated his willingness to testify, although such testimony almost invariably comes about in exchange for a plea bargain; in fact, the prosecution had put together a deal in which Ingram would plead guilty to nine counts of third-degree rape, with the sentences to run concurrently. In return, the prison time would be minimal. There was even a chance that Ingram could walk out of the courtroom a free man once he had testified against his friends.

Ingram confounded everyone by agreeing to testify without making any deals. G. Saxon Rodgers, who was Jim Rabie's attorney, was incredulous—and dismayed. The situation had been a prosecutor's dream, since a jury will usually discount testimony that has been purchased with a plea bargain. Until then Rodgers's theory about the case was that Ingram really had abused his daughters, but in order to mitigate his sentence he had implicated Rabie and Risch, two innocent men. Again and again Ingram had described himself as being a helpless onlooker to the crimes of his friends. He thereby created a conspiracy case in which he would play the role of the key state witness. All this would fit in with the portrait of the cunning, politically sophisticated former deputy sheriff which Rodgers had intended to paint in court. In this rendering, Ingram had controlled the case from the beginning. But when Ingram agreed to testify for nothing, he took the brush out of Rodgers's hand.

On January 30, Sax Rodgers and Richard Cordes, who represented Ray Risch, were permitted to meet with one of the prosecution witnesses. It was Julie. The meeting took place at the Lacey Police Department. Once again, Julie said she hadn't slept in days, and she looked it. She cuddled a stuffed bear that Loreli Thompson had given her, and often didn't respond to questions from the attorneys about the abuse. She seemed to be in a fog. At one point, she crawled under the desk and hid there for ten minutes. When the questioning resumed, Rodgers took a more indirect tack. He asked Julie about Ericka's deceased twin, Andrea. Although they were not identical, they had looked very much alike, except for Andrea's swollen head and the cramped limbs that had confined her to a wheelchair. Julie remembered visiting her at the state institution in Spokane. Sometimes the family would pick up Andrea and take her on vacation to Deer Lake; she wasn't so retarded that she didn't know who they were. Julie remembered her singing the alphabet song and "Jesus Loves Me." Sometimes she had a pointer strapped to her forehead and would pick out tunes on the keyboard. Andrea had died in 1984, just before the twins' eighteenth birthday. Ericka had taken the news very hard; she shut herself up in her room for a month. "A part of me has died," Julie said Ericka had told her.

When the attorneys tried to resume talking about the case, Julie retreated to one-word replies. She spun the stuffed bear in the air. She described Jim Rabie as "Fat. Short. Dark hair. Ugly." She did not know if he had any marks or tattoos. (As it happens, Rabie's chest bears a ropelike, three-inch keloidal scar which was the result of a near-fatal electrocution two decades before. Neither Ingram nor any of the alleged victims had noticed it.) Finally, Cordes asked if Julie would just tell him what his client had done to her. She shrugged.

"Will you ever?" he asked.

"Maybe I will," she responded.

That was the end of the interview. It had taken three and a half hours, and she had said virtually nothing.

A week later, Rodgers and Cordes met with Ericka and the investigators at the sheriff's office. Ericka was far more talkative. She didn't know exactly what happened to Julie or her brothers; in fact, she said that she hadn't known about Julie's abuse or her pregnancy until learning of it from the detectives. She described severe sexual and physical abuse that she herself had suffered, but admitted that she had no permanent scars or marks. She said her mother had been sexually abusing her since she was ten years old; sometimes her father watched, and he would also do things to her when her mother was finished. The last time her mother abused her was in September 1988, when Sandy stuck a closet pole in her vagina. In response to the obvious question of why Ericka would need to reveal the abuse to her mother two months later, if Sandy had been a regular participant in the abuse for more than a decade, Ericka said that everyone had told her this was something she needed to do.

Rodgers finally asked about his client's involvement in these acts, and Ericka told him that Jim Rabie had assaulted her eight times in September alone, and many more times before that—perhaps fifty or a hundred, going back to when she was thirteen. The last time she was assaulted, her father began it, then it was Rabie, then her mother; afterward, each of them defecated on her. As for Risch, she couldn't remember him doing anything sexual to her, except for taking photographs. Usually he just came along to watch.

The prosecutor's attempts to keep the case simple vanished as Ericka elaborated on the satanic rituals before the amazed defense attorneys. She described orgies in the woods, in which babies were sacrificed and buried behind the Ingram house. Rabie and Risch were there, she said. Once, when she was a sophomore in high school, they held her down and tied her to a table. She was pregnant, she said, and someone aborted her baby with a coat hanger. That was very painful. Then the baby was cut up and rubbed all over her body. She had seen approximately twenty-five babies sacrificed over the years.

The defense attorneys could sense panic on the opposing side. The satanic-abuse accusations hadn't hit the press yet, but it was easy to imagine the public outcry when they did, and the pressure that the prosecution would be under to produce convictions. Perhaps all this could be avoided or, at least, contained. The prosecutor, Tabor, might be persuaded to drop the charges against Rabie and Risch if Ingram would quietly plead guilty and get treatment.

Before Tabor would agree to a deal, however, he would have to be persuaded that Rabie and Risch were really innocent men caught up in some kind of familial hysteria. Rabie was still asking for a polygraph test. He knew that polygraphs were not infallible and could not be admitted as evidence, but he had used them repeatedly in his own investigations. He also knew Tabor and the detectives: if Rabie had been in their place, he would have had to think very hard about continuing a prosecution against a man who had willingly taken a lie detector test and passed it.

Early on the morning of February 3, Rabie was taken from his cell in Mason County in chains. He was loaded into a police car and driven to the Olympia Police Department, where Maynard Midthun, an officer Rabie knew, administered the test. It lasted into the afternoon. Several of the investigators watched the procedure on a monitor in another room. They could not forget that Rabie was a former colleague, and that he had been in their place many times. Once again there was that sense of the universe being inverted, as if the entire situation would be revealed as a case of mistaken identity, or a folly of absurdly massive dimensions. It was exactly that rotten odor of comedy that made the Ingram investigation so gruesome, that drew everyone—the detectives, the suspects, the victims—deeper into the macabre.

"Here are the things that will happen here today," Midthun told Rabie. "Initially we're gonna talk about you. . . . Then we'll get into a discussion of the case. Following that, we'll work up some questions that you and I agree are valid questions that will resolve the issue." After that, Rabie would be hooked up to the polygraph and take the test. "This is just another workday for me," Midthun said. "It's your test. Perhaps one of the biggest days in your life."

"Could be," Rabie agreed. He was feeling anxious but confident.

Midthun asked whether Rabie was experiencing any discomfort, and Rabie said he had a toothache and had been suffering constant back pain since he was put in jail. He had taken a sinus pill and something for his digestion the night before, but nothing that should affect the test. The object of this portion of the examination was to put the subject at ease, so Midthun asked Rabie to tell him about his life, particularly his formative years.

"I was raised on a farm," Rabie said. It was a fifty-acre farm in the Yakima Valley, on which Rabie's father raised sugar beets, corn, and hops. The only notable feature of his ancestry was a grandfather who had been hanged for stealing sheep. "I was the eldest child and I had a sister that was eleven months younger than I, and when I was five and she was four we were in an auto wreck. My dad was driving and my sister was killed. My mother was permanently crippled from it. I had a broken leg and a concussion and some head injuries." The cast on the broken leg kept it from growing at the same rate as his good leg, so that limb remained an inch and a half shorter. For the next five years, Rabie was an only child, until his parents adopted another little girl, who was thirteen months old at the time.

It was a rather lonely childhood. The farm was two miles out of town, and there was little to do outside of chores and schoolwork. "I was always overweight and very self-conscious and had no real girlfriends or anything," he recalled. "I'd go to the library. That, to me, was the best thing I could do, and like I said, I didn't socialize much." He was once arrested for driving a car without a license when he was fifteen, but other than that he had never gotten into trouble.

"I really think I had a good childhood," Rabie said, somewhat defensively. He admitted that he didn't really get along with his father, who had a quick temper and had slapped his son on several occasions. The summer Jim graduated from high school, they had a falling out. Jim had complained about his father's coarse eating habits. "He said, 'If you don't like the way I do things, you can move out,' " Rabie recalled. Since he was going away to college anyway, that's exactly what he did.

For the next three and a half years, Jim studied economics and tried to support himself in school. He finally dropped out and began driving a tour bus in Seattle, which he found very satisfying. At the age of twenty-three, he married for the first time, to a schoolteacher. In the meantime, Jim's father had traded the family farm for a general store, which turned out to be a disaster. His father was never cut out for commerce. "It was killing my mother psychologically. She just couldn't stand it," Rabie said. "And so I took over the store and dad got out and I ran it for five years on a shoestring." Jim did everything from the meat cutting to the bookkeeping. Meanwhile, he was commuting forty-five miles every day, each way. "Probably that's what busted up my first marriage," he said. "I was never around."

It was while he was running the store that he electrocuted himself. "I was working on one of the compressor units," he said. He rolled over on an exposed 220-volt wire. He couldn't move off the wire; he couldn't breathe or call out. His body went into convulsions. He remembered hoping that the clerks would know to turn off the power before they touched his body. Then suddenly "it was like a hand picked me up off of there and I went and I passed out in back." In his opinion, it was the hand of God. "I'm not a Bible-pounder by any means," he said, but he did feel that he had been spared, although he didn't know why.

After that experience, Jim sold the store and applied to be in the sheriff's reserves. "I always thought I was too small to be a cop." He happened to be just tall enough. Unexpectedly, he had entered into what he soon decided was his life's calling, law enforcement.

He divorced his first wife in 1977 and started dating Ruth. They had a solid relationship, in his opinion. He depicted his life as being happy and fulfilled—until the Ingram case came along.

"You've painted the model pictures," Midthun said. "I'm challenging you, 'cause I'm also looking for the human side of Jim Rabie, and I'm gonna tell you why. A very important part of this test is 'Who is Jim Rabie?' In fact, it may make up about one-half of our conversation prior to the charts. The other half will be about the case. There, we're gonna talk about some allegations that are very serious, and they could only be accomplished by somebody who is, let us say, a victim himself." The paradigm he was referring to was the common assumption that children who were abused often grow up to be abusers themselves. Rabie would know all the symptoms from his police training, Midthun conceded. One would expect to see a person who has difficulty controlling his anger and who had been abusing other people since childhood. "I'm not doing this for any reason other than to make sure you're painting an accurate picture," said Midthun. "Now, I want the truth, O.K.? That model child was a model child, perhaps—very bright, very good grade point, good anger control—but we all have our transgressions. Tell me some of the dirt, Jim."

"I've thought about going into anger-control counseling," Rabie admitted. "In my normal life I have no problem with anger control. Those that are very close to me, I can get very angry with—verbally, not physically."

"Does it ever turn out to be malicious?" asked Midthun. "Have you found yourself to be vindictive?"

"When provoked, and my anger is really high, I can be vindictive, yes," Rabie agreed.

"Have you ever been a victim of abuse?"

"Never physical abuse, but I do feel that I was a bit of a victim of my father's mental abuse."

When Midthun asked him if he had ever been in a fistfight, Rabie said that he had gotten his nose bloodied by a schoolmate back when he was in high school. "All I did was grab him, because I'm not a boxer, and he came up a couple days later and apologized to me, and we've been pretty good friends since then."

"What you just described to me is a textbook description of somebody who is normal," said Midthun. "Is it true?"

"Yeah, that's what happened."

"Somebody who is acting out, who is gonna place blame someplace other than where it belongs—like, on themselves— they're gonna blame others for their problems," Midthun observed. "I mean, they would retaliate. It would be one of those things where years after that fight they would still be holding a grudge. They would be still looking for a way to get even, and here you're telling me this guy has become a friend. . . . Doesn't it make sense that only somebody who is very comfortable with hurting other people could commit the type of crimes that you're accused of?"

"Yeah, I guess," Rabie said. "I hadn't looked at it that way in the whole case."

"In those formative years, was there ever any sexual acting out?" Midthun asked. "I'm looking at sexual deviancy. . . . I'm not talking about getting your hands on a *Playboy* magazine when you're thirteen years old."

Rabie admitted that he had masturbated frequently, but otherwise his lifetime sexual experience was confined to five women. He said he was once tempted by a prostitute, but he was broke at the time.

This all seemed so normal—bland even, almost Victorian. "The person that was just described to me has no ties to these deplorable acts," Midthun said. Why, then, did Rabie think he had been charged with these crimes?

"Because Brian has a big hard-on for me."

"Brian?"

"Schoening. Brian brought my name into this. Paul was searching for the individual to hang it on," Rabie explained, giving his version of events. Having studied the police reports and transcripts of some of the interviews, and having heard some of the department gossip, Rabie pointed out that Julie initially had implicated her father, an uncle, and a friend of her father's. "She was asked if the friend was still around, and her response was, 'Probably,' which would exclude me, 'cause she knew I was around, and it would exclude Ray Risch, which is my closest friend, 'cause she had ridden with him less than a month before that." When Paul was first questioned and started naming friends who might be involved, he kept visualizing someone big. All the other men he named were over six feet, but for some reason Schoening kept bringing Rabie's name back into the discussion. Then, when Julie was shown the photo lineup, the only ones she knew by name were Rabie and Risch. "I think Paul is really enjoying that he is running the sheriff's department ragged on a case that could've been over very quickly," said Rabie. "I actually have had almost minimal contact with the girls or the kids—any of the kids. I can't even tell you what Ericka looks like."

Then why was Rabie so ambivalent when he was first questioned about his involvement in the case? He claimed that the detectives had never hinted at the extent of the charges; he thought they were talking about a sexual molestation, such as inappropriate touching, that might even have been unintentional or have taken place while he was intoxicated. "They're talking about a molest that occurred in the seventies, and they're not very specific; they're telling some things about a picture and [being] nude, but they're not saying what I'm doing, exactly. . . . I do start doubting my own memory if you've got a whole string of people telling that I've been doing this, and you've got photographs." Since he learned the nature of the charges and the span of time they were supposed to have covered, he no longer believed that he could have blocked the events out of his mind.

At this point, Midthun began preparing the four questions that would make up the heart of the test. He reviewed some of the charges that Ericka and Julie had made against Rabie, which were clearly not accidental touching or incidental molestations but savage, chronic abuse. He would ask a question concerning each of the girls to determine whether Rabie had ever had sexual contact with them. Another question would be whether Rabie had threatened the Ingram children. "For the sake of the test, we don't care about Paul and we don't care about Sandy, because they're adults," said Midthun; in any case, Rabie had not been charged with any crimes concerning the parents. A final question, which Midthun said would enhance the reliability of the test, would be whether Rabie intended to respond truthfully. Midthun then took a bathroom break and came back to wire the suspect to the polygraph machine.

The lie detector is both a crude and a fragile instrument. It has been used by police departments since 1924 and has changed little since that time. Midthun strapped two corrugated rubber tubes around Rabie's midsection, one across his upper chest and one just above his stomach, over his diaphragm. These pneumatic tubes led to a bellows that recorded the expansion of the lungs with each breath. He then placed a cardiac cuff, such as medical technicians use to take blood pressure, around

Rabie's upper right arm, and inflated it to more than eighty pounds of pressure—somewhat higher than normal, to account for Rabie's moderate corpulence. Finally, he attached metal plates around Rabie's left index and ring fingers with Velcro straps. These tiny plates measured the galvanic skin response (GSR), which is, essentially, the reaction of the sweat glands to the minuscule amount of electric current running through the plates. Moisture coming into contact with the current would produce a measurable response.

The information gathered by these devices is recorded on a continuously moving graph. Normal breathing appears as a wavy line of gentle hills and valleys. The blood pressure is represented by a series of spikes reflecting the constrictions of the heart. The GSR is a narrower, undulating line. In each case, there is a commonsense understanding of the reaction that is being gauged: a person says, "I caught my breath," or "My heart pounded," or "I broke out in a cold sweat." It is exactly these kinds of stress responses that the polygraph records. Of the three, the GSR demonstrates the most dramatic reaction, sometimes producing wild swings across the graph that look like angry scribbles, but respiration is thought to be the most significant indicator. People who are trying to cheat the polygraph will sometimes hold their breath or take drugs that suppress their reactions. In fact, people can be trained to beat the polygraph through rather minute actions such as flexing one's toes or biting one's tongue. Coughing, sighing, or simply shifting one's weight in the chair can produce reactions, which is why the polygraph operator must constantly observe the subject and note on the chart each time the person swallows or takes a deep breath. The startled reaction to a ringing telephone looks like an earthquake on the graph.

What is actually being detected is not deception but anxiety. The philosophy behind the machine is that lying is inherently conflictual. That's not true for everyone, however;

sociopaths who don't appear to suffer the ordinary pangs of conscience may lie without registering measurable stress on the polygraph. Moreover, people who are genuinely deluded will appear to be telling the truth even if what they are saying is beyond possibility. Some studies have shown that polygraphs are accurate only 64 to 71 percent of the time when used in criminal investigations. The most common error is to mistake innocent subjects as guilty, rather than vice versa. For all of these reasons, polygraphs are generally not allowed in court, and limitations have been placed on their use by private employers.

Many law-enforcement officers, however, believe that in the hands of an experienced operator, such as Maynard Midthun, the polygraph is close to being infallible. Jim Rabie believed this when he was a cop. Midthun offered the example of two men accused of a bank robbery. One is guilty, the other innocent. Each has been identified by an eyewitness. Each convincingly denies his involvement. "We don't know if they're telling the truth," said Midthun. There is a difference between the two suspects, however. "The guy who really did it," Midthun explains, offering a commonplace understanding of the nature of memory, "he experiences distinct physiological changes that take place when he walks through the front door of that bank, and he pulls out that weapon and sticks it in the face of that teller. . . . It's as though somebody has turned on a video camera in his mind. . . . There is a permanent record there of the words spoken, the deeds done, the emotions felt—it's all there, recorded." The innocent man, on the other hand, hasn't had the experience. There's no tape playing in his head. Three years after the bank robbery, both men come in for polygraphs. The innocent man denies he robbed the bank. "What I see on the polygraph charts is general nervous tension, and it's that way throughout the entire chart. One question does not mean any more to him than any of the others, because it's the same. He has no frame of reference. He never spoke those words. He never did that deed." When the guilty man takes the same test, however, "at that point, the video camera clicks on. The camera's been off for three years, except when he wanted to reflect back on how fun it was and how cool he was for getting away with it. But when we go into the polygraph test, he cannot push the off switch. He cannot turn that son of a gun off. . . . I ask the question, 'Did you rob the bank?' The camera is playing and he sees an instant replay of himself entering the bank, sticking his nose in the teller's face, and watching her just totally lose control. He'll never forget that. . . . There's that adrenaline rush. Then he flunks the test."

Because of his experience in the use of the polygraph, Rabie may have realized that harboring secret guilty thoughts about one's past actions can cause false reactions; for instance, the innocent person who is accused of robbing the bank might register a highly anxious reaction if he had done something similar in the past. That's why polygraph operators spend several hours before the test trying to determine areas of conflict; it's also why the questions must be made as specific as possible. In any case, as he was being wired to the machine Rabie suddenly felt the need to clear his conscience. It turned out that his sexual life had not been unblemished, after all; he admitted to several indiscretions, the most serious being an incident that happened when he was thirteen and he was playing with a four-year-old girl. "I don't remember exactly the circumstances," Rabie said, fumbling over his words, "but I ended up—I know I had my penis between her legs—didn't try to enter her in any manner, but between her legs."

"Let's chalk that one up to one of life's experiences," Midthun said forgivingly. "What I would be interested in is if you went back for seconds, because that would begin to make a pattern, right? One time does not make a pattern. The true pedophile, the person who would do the horrible things that the Ingram family has complained about, has a pattern of un-natural acts.''

To establish a controlled lie as a base for measurement, Midthun had Rabie write the numeral 7 on a piece of paper. He then instructed him to respond ''No'' when asked if he had written the numerals 4, 5, or 6, which was an honest response; then say ''No'' for 7, which was a lie; then ''No'' again for 8 and 9. Midthun would then have what he called ''a perfect picture of a lie, much like the bank robber tells, surrounded by nervous truthful responses, much like the innocent person.'' Rabie's GSR barely registered when he lied about the 7, but his heartbeat jumped off the chart. Midthun had to adjust the pen to keep it on the graph.

Midthun then began the test, mixing in irrelevant questions with the four key questions that were designed to determine whether Rabie was guilty or innocent.

''Is your first name James?''

''Yes,'' said Rabie.

''You were born in the month of May?''

''Yes.''

''Regarding sexual contact with the Ingram children, do you intend to answer truthfully?'' This was Midthun's first key question.

''Yes!'' Rabie said loudly.

''Is today Friday?''

''Yes.''

''Have you ever had any sexual contact with Julie?'' This was the second key question.

''No.''

''Other than what you've told me about, between the ages of twelve and thirty, did you ever take part in an unnatural sex act?''

''No.''

''Do you sometimes watch television?''

"Yes."

"Did you have any sexual contact with Ericka?" The third key question.

"No."

"Have you ever threatened any of the Ingram children?" The fourth key question.

"No."

"Before the age of thirty, did you ever intentionally hurt anyone?"

"No."

Midthun performed the test three times to make certain of Rabie's responses. In each of the four relevant questions, the graph showed that Rabie had lied.

11

———

$\mathbf{D}$etective Brian Schoening was waiting at the Seattle-Tacoma International Airport on the morning of February 2 to pick up Dr. Richard Ofshe, a social psychologist from the University of California at Berkeley. Ofshe had been recommended to the prosecution as an expert on cults and mind control. With his dark, owlish eyes and a luxuriant gray-white beard that lent him an air of Zeus-like authority, Ofshe certainly looked the part of a distinguished professor. Brainy, arrogant, long-winded, precise, insightful, prickly, and self-promoting, the forty-seven-year-old Ofshe had all the faults and virtues of the academic genius, as well as a taste for fine food, fast cars, and heated controversy. His credentials included a Pulitzer Prize, which he shared in 1979, for research and reporting on the Synanon cult in Southern California. He had written extensively about how the thought-control techniques developed in Communist China, the Soviet Union, and North Korea had come to be employed and refined by various religious cults in the United States. His research had caused him to become involved in a number of lawsuits against the Unification Church, the Church of Scientology, and est, to name a few. His critics called him an anti-cult extremist; they believed that his campaign against cults could as easily be turned against organized, established religions. But few cared to take on Richard Ofshe directly; his appetite for intellectual combat was matched only by his stubbornness.

Gary Tabor had been looking for some expert who could explain what appeared to be the mind-controlled behavior of virtually everyone in the Ingram case, suspects and victims alike. He had called Ofshe and asked if he had much experience with satanic cults. Ofshe had told him candidly that no one could really claim to be an expert, because so far such allegations were largely unproved. This is real, Tabor had assured him. Then I'm interested, Ofshe had replied.

As they drove to Olympia, Schoening briefed the professor on the case. Practically nothing that anyone was saying could be verified. All the stories were at war with each other. People weren't even talking normally, Schoening complained. Ofshe asked what he meant by that, and Schoening described Ingram's third-person confessions in which Ingram saw himself from the outside, as if the Ingram who was watching and the Ingram who was acting were two different people. He mentioned the "would've"s and "must have"s that characterized Ingram's language. As for the daughters, they talked little, if at all.

The problem everyone had was Paul's continuing inability to remember clearly. That struck a familiar chord with Ofshe. In addition to his work with cults, he had interested himself in coercive police interrogations. At that moment, he had a paper in press with the *Cultic Studies Journal* concerning innocent people who became convinced of their guilt and confessed. In each case that Ofshe had studied, the confession had come about when the police succeeded in persuading the suspect that the evidence against him was overwhelming and that if he couldn't remember committing the crime, there was a valid reason for his lack of memory, such as his having blocked it out or fallen into some kind of fugue state.

In the Ingram case, Ofshe was told, the reason the suspect couldn't remember raping his children repeatedly over seventeen years was that he had repressed the memories as soon as the abuse occurred. Even the prosecution was uncomfortable with that theory, and the notion of mind control had arisen as an alternative to it. Perhaps the cult had interfered with the ordinary process of memory formation, through drugs or chronic abuse. Perhaps the reputedly brilliant Dr. Ofshe could unlock the programming that had scrambled the circuitry of nearly everyone in the Ingram family.

Ofshe's first interview was with Paul Ingram, in the presence of Schoening and Vukich. He was impressed by Ingram's eagerness to help and his longing to understand his own confused state of mind. As Ofshe tried to get Ingram to lead him through the case, however, he decided that there was clearly something wrong. In Ofshe's opinion, it wasn't possible for the human memory to operate in the fashion that Ingram was describing. Either he was lying or he was deluded. When Ofshe asked him to describe more routine episodes in his life, Ingram demonstrated perfectly ordinary recall. Then where were those other memories coming from? Ingram described the manner in which he would get an image and then pray on it. He told Ofshe he had been practicing a relaxation technique he had read about in a magazine, in which he would imagine going into a warm white fog. Minutes would pass and then more images would come, he said, and he felt confident that they were real memories because Pastor Bratun had assured him that God would bring him only the truth. After a while, he would write his memories down. Ofshe wondered if Ingram was possibly taking a daydream and recoding it as a memory. He made a spontaneous decision to run what he later referred to as a "little experiment" to determine whether Ingram was lying or believed that what he was relating was genuine.

"I was talking to one of your sons and one of your daughters, and they told me about something that happened," Ofshe said to Ingram, giving a wink to Schoening and Vukich. The two detectives looked at him in complete dumbfounded surprise, since Ofshe had not yet met any other members of the Ingram family. "It was about a time when you made them have sex with each other while you watched. Do you remember that?"

No, Ingram didn't remember that. In fact, the detectives had posed a similar scenario to him in his first round of interviews, when he was confessing to a number of crimes, and he had not remembered it then, either. But Ofshe was not deterred. "This really did happen," he insisted. "Your children were there—they both remember it. Why can't you?"

Ingram wanted to know where it had happened.

"It happened in the new house," Schoening said, playing along.

Ingram closed his eyes and put his head in his hands, a familiar posture to the detectives. Several minutes passed.

"I can kind of see Ericka and Paul Ross," Ingram said.

Ofshe told him not to say any more. Go back to your cell and pray on it, he said.

When Ingram left the interview room, the detectives jumped down Ofshe's throat. What was he up to? Ofshe explained that he was simply testing the validity of Ingram's memories. In that case, they asked, why couldn't he have picked something a little further out of the realm of possibility? None of the investigators would have been surprised if Ingram had orchestrated sex among his children—that wasn't any more bizarre or depraved than the stories they had already heard.

Later that afternoon, Ofshe met Julie at the sheriff's office, in the company of Detective Thompson, Gary Tabor, and Julie's advocate from a local rape crisis center. Julie turned her chair around and faced the wall, communicating mainly through nods of her head.

Despite this awkward arrangement, Ofshe thought he detected a certain playfulness in Julie. He hoped he could use it to draw her out. For the first time, Julie produced cult memories of her own. She wrote a brief description of people in robes and a doll hanging from a tree. Ofshe asked if the members of the cult had told her they had magic powers. "No, they didn't," Julie said. Did anyone ever tell her that the cult knew what she was doing all the time? There was no answer. Was that a question she didn't want to answer? The back of Julie's head nodded. "That means it's true, then," Ofshe said. He asked Julie to write down how they were able to spy on her. Julie wrote, "They said that a high and mighty man spoke to them and would tell them ever thing I said, or did. The high & mighty man spoke to them threw other people." Was that high and mighty man the Devil? Julie shrugged. Had she ever seen any bad things done to animals? She shook her head no. To babies? No. Dolls? Yes, Julie indicated, and wrote: "They would hang dolls with blood on the trees and say the white lady would kill them and who kill you if you told." She didn't know who the white lady was, but she wrote that the woman wore "a long white dress like a costume." Julie talked of having gone to church frequently when she was a child and having liked it "some." She believed in Satan but did not know why. She described herself as being a weird and nervous person. Ofshe asked her to write the names of any other children in the cult. She wrote down "Ericka, Chad, Paul," and the names of three other children—names that had not previously come up. Then she listed the adults, again mentioning new names. For the first time, the membership of the cult was taking shape. As far as the investigators were concerned, it was a highly productive interview. They were amazed at how much information Ofshe had been able to get out of Julie.

The contrast between the sisters struck Ofshe strongly

when, the next day, he met Ericka. Julie was such a casual dresser—to the point, really, of being careless—whereas Ericka was heavily made up and wore her hair teased into a dramatic coif. Instead of shrinking from the spotlight, Ericka seemed eager to claim center stage. The sisters scarcely seemed related at all, except as opposites: Julie so shy, Ericka so bold; Julie so plain and naive, Ericka so attractive and shrewd.

Until now, the interrogation of the girls had focused on the commission of crimes. Ofshe chose another tack. He proposed to Ericka that he was like an anthropologist who had just dropped into her town and was interested in learning about her life in the cult. Tell me what the meetings were like, how they fitted into your ordinary life, he said. It was similar to the approach he had used in debriefing members of other cults. In such organizations there is a hierarchy of personalities; there are routines, taboos, maxims, legends, dogma, group history—a society, in other words. By her own estimate, Ericka had attended eight hundred and fifty rituals during her life and watched twenty-five babies sacrificed. What, exactly, went on during the rituals? Ofshe wanted to know. "They chant," Ericka said. What were the words? She couldn't remember. Did you sit or stand? he asked her. She couldn't remember that either. Who were the other people and what were they like? It was too stressful to talk about. Before concluding the interview, Ofshe asked if her father had ever forced her and one of her brothers to have sex while he watched. Ericka said that nothing like that had ever happened.

That day Ofshe visited Ingram again, in jail. Ingram said he had gotten some clear memories of Ericka and Paul Ross having sex. He had made some notes. Once again, Ofshe asked him to say no more, just go back to his cell and pray and visualize and write it down for him.

Ofshe also met with Sandy. She told him that she was be-

ginning to retrieve more memories now, through the counseling of Pastor Bratun. She had also seen a psychiatrist and a
psychologist.

"How does Pastor Bratun help?" Ofshe asked.

"He kind of prods," Sandy said. "When we start, initially
he did describe a scene to me."

"One that Paul had given him?" asked Ofshe.

Sandy agreed that most of her memory sessions began this
way.

Ofshe wanted to know if Sandy was afraid of her husband.

"No," she said. "I remember him hollering at me sometimes, in my normal memory, but it was never anything that
seemed out of line. I remember him hitting me one time, in
my normal memory, but I don't remember anything that
would have given me a clue that something was wrong."

"Where did you get this idea of a normal memory and
some other kind of memory?" Ofshe asked.

"There are things I remember, like birthday parties and
how old the kids were in this particular year," Sandy said.
"Then there are the things that I've remembered since then.
It is different from what my other memories are."

Ofshe asked her to describe the memories she was getting
with the help of Pastor Bratun. Sandy detailed several rape
scenes with Rabie and Risch, and satanic rituals in the woods.
She watched Paul having sex with the high priestess. "I remember being tied to a tree," she said. "There was water and
fire. One time, Jim took the kids by their heels and dumped
them in the water. And they wanted me to put on a white
robe. . . . Ray's standing out there and he's holding all the
robes, and when I first saw the scene it felt like an initiation."

"Do you 'see' the scene, or do you remember it?"

"No, I see it," Sandy said. "And, uh, everybody says this
pledge of allegiance and we're all outside, and there's this book

on the table and, uh, Jim is holding my shoulder and his nails are all painted black and they're real long and they go into my shoulder and this book is *bleeding*"—her voice broke, and she began to sob—"and Paul and [the high priestess]* and Jim touch it, and the blood runs all over Jim and up his arm and all over his head and then it runs all over me!"

"So the blood runs uphill?"

Sandy laughed despairingly. "Jim says I am ready, and they put me on the table, and there's like a leather strap around my neck and my arms and my legs and my ankles, and then [the high priestess] cuts my clothes off with the knife!"

By now Sandy was shaking. Everyone who had seen her when she was caught up in this state had been alarmed by her bobbing head, her rolling eyes, and her high, quaking voice. Her face became bizarrely contorted. When Sax Rodgers deposed her, it had been one of the most rattling experiences of his life. Even Loreli Thompson had been unnerved by the eerie spectacle that Sandy presented.

Ofshe now pulled her back by getting her to describe ordinary memories, such as family vacations. She immediately calmed down. She talked about trips to Deer Lake in eastern Washington, and picking up Andrea beforehand, and other times, when the kids were small and they would all go camping and take long walks together. "There was a little store there, and paddle boats, and the kids could fish off the dock and swim."

"Do you remember those things?" Ofshe asked.

"Yes."

"Can you remember them without 'seeing' them?"

---

*The name of the woman referred to as the high priestess, as well as the names of other persons who were implicated in the investigation but who were not charged, are not part of this account.

"Yes."

"Can you remember the other kinds of scenes without 'seeing' them?"

"I don't know. I just see 'em, that's all," Sandy said. "I can feel them touching me and holding me. I can smell things."

"So it's real for you."

Sandy agreed that it was very real.

"Would it surprise you if I told you that I think nothing happened?" Ofshe asked.

"Well, we've talked about that," Sandy admitted. "I've even thought about that myself—you know, that this was all a big lie and a hoax."

"Those aren't the words I would use," Ofshe said gently. "If I told you I thought this had all come about by mistake, would that surprise you?"

"Well," Sandy said, "everything that's happened has been very surprising and very strange, but I'd wonder why I was feeling them touching me, holding me, and I could smell them, feel them, and hear them."

"Do you have bad dreams like this?"

"No," Sandy said. "There'd have to be another explanation—or else you can just put me away! And I don't think I'm crazy."

To everyone's astonishment, Paul Ross had returned to Olympia for a spell, and Ofshe managed to interview him as well. Like the detectives, Ofshe was struck by the air of dangerousness that surrounded the young man. Paul Ross related the same story that he had told before, about his mother being tied to the bed while Rabie raped her, and his father hitting him. He described his father as a "Dr. Jekyll and Mr. Hyde" personality. His mother, on the other hand, "always seemed to be the loving, caring mom," but after what his sisters had said about her, Paul Ross supposed she must have been involved in the abuse. He guessed she too must have a separate personality.

Paul Ross said he didn't know anything about the satanic rites that had supposedly gone on in his family, except what he had read in the newspaper, and yet he was quite learned on the subject of demonology, a subject he had been studying for the past ten years. He had read Aleister Crowley, the Egyptian *Book of the Dead*, and many of the most significant books on witchcraft, satanism, magic, and voodoo. As a professor, Ofshe admired Paul Ross's scholarship, and he was frustrated that this angry but nonetheless quite studious young man was working in a warehouse. He several times took the opportunity to recommend that Paul Ross apply to college, and even offered to advise him.

"I would like to touch on whether or not anything at all was done to you," Ofshe then said cautiously, "and whether or not you were ever part of any group sessions that had any aspect of ritual."

"First of all, I don't know," Paul Ross responded. "And second, I don't remember anything." When Ofshe asked him to explain, the young man said he had no clear memories before he was eight years old, although after talking to detectives he recalled that he had fallen down the stairs a lot. "Either I was really clumsy, or somebody did a lot of pushing. I remember one time waking up in the hospital after they had shaved the back of my head. It seems like I should remember falling down the stairs." This happened when he was four or five years old. He still had a scar. But as for being present at satanic rituals all through his childhood, Paul Ross said, "I couldn't say yes or no. I don't remember anything."

Like everyone else in the case, Ofshe was perplexed by Paul Ross's story. It was so suggestive but also so unconfirming. Did the abuse happen? The young man believed it must have, but he couldn't remember it; nor could he remember the rituals. The only thing he clearly recalled was Rabie's assault on Sandy. And yet, Ofshe felt if that part of Paul Ross's story was actually true, then everything else the family remembered—even the most fantastic ritual scenes—must be true as well.

The next time Ofshe visited Ericka, she said she believed that her mother was still a member of the cult. She related a recent incident in which Sandy had come to visit her at the house of Pastor Ron Long and had given her the cult's "death kiss." Ofshe asked her to describe it. What made it different from an ordinary kiss? Ericka couldn't say. When Ofshe later asked the pastor and his wife if they had seen Sandy kiss Ericka, what they described was an ordinary peck on the cheek.

Ofshe now saw Paul Ingram for a third time. Schoening recognized the look on Ingram's face when he came into the interview room. He was beaming. Ingram was always proud of himself after he had come up with a new memory. He handed Ofshe a three-page written confession. Ofshe read it through. "Daytime: Probably Saturday or Sunday Afternoon," the confession began, very much like a movie script:

> In Ericka's Bedroom on Fir Tree. Bunk Beds set up. Ericka & Julie are sharing the room. I ask or tell Paul Jr. & Ericka to come upstairs & then we go into Ericka's room. I close the door and tell them we are going to play (a game?).
>
> I tell them to undress. Ericka says "But Dad", I say "Just get undressed and don't argue" From my tone or the way I say it, neither objects and they undress themselves. I'm probably blocking the door so they could not get out.
>
> Ericka is about 12–13. Body fairly well developed. Paul is 12–14. Both have some pubic hair.
>
> I tell Ericka to knell and to caress Paul's genitals. When erect I tell her to put the penis into her mouth and to orally stimulate him. I also tell her to continue using her fingers. I have her also run her tongue along his penis. When Paul has

his orgasm I have Ericka hold his penis in her mouth and continue stimulation. I tell her to swallow the sperm, but she runs to the bathroom and spits. I tell her to get back to the room & tell her the sperm is protein and won't hurt her.

I have Ericka lie on her back on the floor. I tell Paul to knell over her to rub her vagina gently with his fingers. I also tell him to caress and touch her breasts. When he has a full erection I tell him to enter Ericka and complete the sex act. When they are finished, I have Ericka clean up and tell her to come back to the bedroom.

I undress and tell Ericka to orally have sex with me. She does what I tell her to do. That is to stimulate me with her fingers, tongue and mouth until I come. I tell her to catch sperm in her mouth, and she can swallow or spit. I believe she spits in the bathroom.

I have her lie on the floor. I caress her vagina and breasts and probably orally caress her vagina. I have vaginal sex. Paul watches all of this. If she did not have an orgasm I would have stimulated her with my fingers until she did.

I may have told the children that they needed to learn the sex acts and how to do them right. That it is important that each participant have a pleasurable experience.

I may have anal sex with Paul, not real clear. At other times I have had anal and oral sex with him.

We all get dressed. I ask "Now you both enjoyed that didn't you?" Neither looks me in the eye, nor says anything. I say "You might as well enjoy it. We need each other, there's no reason to fight it."

Paul goes downstairs. I go to my bedroom, perhaps to clean up, Ericka stays in her room. I go downstairs. Sandy and the other children are down there. I go to Sandy in the kitchen and kiss her as if nothing has happened. Nothing is said about what just happened. I don't think Sandy is aware of what went on.

I'm not sure how often this type of activity occurred. I believe that I tell them to be gentle with each other.

I believe that when I tell Paul & Ericka to come upstairs, those on the main floor who heard me and Paul & Ericka, knew what was going on and not to interrupt us.

The ability to control Paul & Ericka may not come entirely from me. It seems there is a real fear of Jim or someone else. Someone may have told me to do this with the kids. This is a feeling I have.

Here was a detailed, explicit confession, complete with dialogue, of a scene that never happened. So far, Ofshe's little experiment had demonstrated just how much pressure it took to make Ingram comply with his demands to create a memory, and the answer was scarcely any. The next task was to determine whether Ingram now would admit that the confession was false. But in this, Paul was unshakable. "It's just as real to me as anything else," he maintained.

Ofshe now had serious doubts whether Ingram was guilty of anything, except of being a highly suggestible individual with a tendency to float in and out of trance states and a patent and rather dangerous eagerness to please authority. He suspected Ericka of being a habitual liar. Throughout the investigation, Julie's accusations had followed Ericka's lead. Ofshe doubted whether the sisters had ever intended their charges to be drawn into the legal arena. Once the charges had been filed, Ofshe believed, the sisters pasted over the inconsistencies in their original accusations with ever more fanciful claims. The whole misadventure was a kind of mass folly—something that would be suitable mainly for folklorists if it were not that innocent people's lives were being crushed. When Ofshe left Olympia, he was convinced that a new Salem was in the making. The witch trials, he believed, were about to begin.

12

———

Chris listens to his older brother, Jim, talk about how Chris was lost in a shopping mall when he was five years old. "It was 1981 or 1982. I remember that Chris was five. We had gone shopping at the University City shopping mall in Spokane. After some panic, we found Chris being led down the mall by a tall, oldish man (I think he was wearing a flannel shirt). Chris was crying and holding the man's hand. The man explained that he had found Chris walking around, crying his eyes out, just a few moments before and was trying to help him find his parents."

This scene comes from an experiment conducted by Elizabeth F. Loftus, a professor of psychology at the University of Washington in Seattle. It was part of a study to determine whether false memories can be implanted and come to be believed with the same assuredness with which one believes real memories. Chris, who is fourteen, has no memory of ever being lost in a shopping mall, but when he is told this story by a person he regards as an authority—his older brother—his usual resistance to influence falls away. Just two days later, when Chris is asked to recall being lost, he has already attached feelings to this nonevent: "That day, I was so scared that I would never see my family again. I knew that I was in trouble." The next day, he remembers that his mother told him never to do that again. On the fourth day, he recalls the old man's flannel shirt. By day five, he can see the stores in the mall. He can even recollect fragments of conversation with the old man. When Chris is finally told by his older brother that the lost-in-the-mall memory is false, he is shaken: "Really? I thought I remembered being lost . . . and looking around for you guys. I do remember that. And then crying, and Mom coming up and saying, 'Where were you? Don't you—don't you ever do that again.' "

Dr. George Ganaway, who has written extensively about the effect of hypnosis on memory, performed a related experiment that was inspired by Loftus's research. He asked a highly hypnotizable subject to allow him to make a suggestion to her while she was in a trance state. The suggestion was that between the time she left the shopping mall and arrived home there were five missing hours. Could she account for the time? The subject began to tell a story about driving past a ranch and stopping to help a cow deliver a calf. Ganaway, who admits he was looking for something more exotic, added the detail that there was a bright light overhead. At once the woman recalled that there was a great noise, and she looked up to see a UFO. Both the woman and the newly born calf were taken up by aliens.

"Did they experiment on you?" Ganaway asked.

"No."

"Try harder," he suggested.

"Oh, yes," she suddenly remembered, and then began to unfold an elaborate abduction drama, which spiraled back into an earlier time in her life when she had also been abducted. She then recalled a near-death experience and kept regressing until she entered a past life in eighteenth-century England, when she was living in a castle. All of this unfolded from the hypothesis that there was a gap in her day for which she needed to make an accounting.

When the subject came out of her trance, Ganaway asked what she recalled. She remembered only delivering the calf, which she knew didn't happen. She was shocked when he showed her a video of herself producing these statements, but upon reflection she was able to describe the daily experiences that formed the raw material of these fantasies. For instance, in the trance the subject said that the aliens had taken a tissue sample that had left a cloverleaf scar. As it happened, the day before she had been wrapping a clover leaf as a present. The eighteenth-century British lady complained of having to "sew, sew, sew," and the subject had just completed sewing a dress for her daughter.

Even stranger than these confabulated memories was the fact that during the next year the subject had repeated flashbacks of the images she had conjured up in the trance. Several days after the experiment, for instance, she was driving past a billboard advertising Bugle Boy jeans and suddenly had a vision of being in the alien spacecraft. These flashbacks happened despite the fact that she knew the images were fantasies and had been produced in an experiment; they still clung to her memory with the tenacity of real events.

Other experiments have demonstrated how unreliable memories are for things as trivial as whom people voted for in the last election or where they were when the shuttle *Challenger* exploded. After a sniper attack at an elementary school playground, children who were not at school when the attack occurred developed memories of witnessing the event. Loftus quotes one government study of 590 persons known to have been in an injury-producing automobile accident; approximately 14 percent had forgotten the event a year later. In another example, 1,500 people who had been discharged from a hospital during the preceding year were asked about the experience; more than a fourth did not remember being hospitalized.

The research that Loftus and others have been conducting on memory threatens many of the most deeply held convictions of psychology—most prominently, the concept of repression, "the cornerstone," as Sigmund Freud wrote in 1914, "on which the whole structure of psychoanalysis rests." The theory has it that, like denial—which pushes aside painful thoughts that are a part of the present—the act of repression blocks painful or conflictual memories of past events from gaining consciousness. These repressed memories, feelings, wishes, or desires lurk in the unconscious and may cause a person to act in an irrational and apparently self-defeating manner. If a child, for instance, is angry at his father but has repressed this feeling, he may express his rage by breaking the law. Thus, when Chad Ingram was caught clumsily trying to shoplift some Christmas candy when he was seventeen years old and went to jail in handcuffs, it was "the proudest moment of my life." The whole point of psychoanalysis is to bring repressed material into conscious awareness, where it can be identified and disarmed.

According to the repression theory, patients may be expected to recover memories of childhood trauma in therapy, although on occasion such memories may simply pop into consciousness as a result of being cued by something in the surroundings. A woman named Eileen Franklin was playing with her five-year-old daughter in San Mateo, California, in 1989 when she suddenly recalled the expression on the face of a childhood friend who had been murdered twenty years before. In therapy, more fragments of that memory returned. She remembered having seen her father sexually assaulting her friend in the back of a Volkswagen van and later crushing her friend's skull with a rock. This, at least, is the story she told on the witness stand. Franklin earlier had told her brother and mother that the memory had come to her while she was under hypnosis. The state of California does not admit hypnotically enhanced recollections. By the time she got to court, she had changed her account several times. She said that she had retrieved the image in a dream, then that it had come to her in therapy, and finally that it had come in the flashback she had while looking at her daughter. That is the statement she later told the jury. Based primarily on Franklin's description of the recovered memory, her father was convicted of murder in the first degree.* He is now serving a life sentence in San Quentin prison.

Similarly, when Frank Fitzpatrick, a thirty-eight-year-old insurance adjuster in Rhode Island, found himself in great mental pain and could not understand the cause of such anguish, he lay on his bed and began to remember the sound of heavy breathing. "Then I realized I had been sexually abused by someone I loved," Fitzpatrick later told the *New York Times*. Eventually, he was able to put a name to his abuser: Father James Porter, who had been his priest in North Attleboro, Massachusetts, three decades before. "Remember Father Porter?" Fitzpatrick asked in an ad he placed in newspapers in 1989, as part of a search for other victims. More than a hundred people have since come forward. Most of them had never forgotten the abuse; for a small number of others, there was a sudden realization, when they heard about the case on the radio or on television, that it had happened to them.†

Public awareness of recovered memories of abuse increased with the 1991 revelation by Roseanne Arnold that she remembered being sexually abused by her mother, from infancy to

---

*For an insightful account of this fascinating case, see *Once Upon a Time* by Harry N. MacLean (HarperCollins, 1993).

†Initial reports suggested that 20 percent of the Father Porter victims had repressed their memories of the event; however, Dr. Stuart Grassion, a psychiatrist who evaluated the victims, says that the figure is closer to 5 percent.

age seven. The same year, Marilyn Van Derbur, a former Miss America, said she had repressed memories of childhood sexual abuse by her father until she was twenty-four years old. Loreli Thompson has never had the experience of having repressed memories suddenly surface in her own mind, but she gets calls all the time from people, mainly women, who do remember abuse and want to know whether they can prosecute. In most cases, the statute of limitations for criminal proceedings has expired; however, changes in legislation in several states, Washington among them, have adjusted the statute of limitations for civil litigation, so that suits can be brought within three years of the date the abuse is *remembered*, regardless of when it was committed. A number of survivor self-help books, such as *The Courage to Heal*, advocate bringing suits against perpetrators, who are usually the victim's parents. Such actions can be very difficult to defend, given the passage of time, and terribly expensive, while the plaintiff can often obtain a lawyer on the promise of a contingency fee. Moreover, if the victim can't afford therapy, the state will pay for it, and this has led critics to charge that both therapists and clients have an incentive to search for memories of abuse that may not have happened.*
In any case, recently there has been a flood of accusations based on recovered memories. Many of these memories are of satanic-ritual abuse.

The concept of repression is so deeply fixed in the culture that few question its factual basis. "Remembering Incest &

---

*Washington was the first state to allow recovered memory claims under the crime victims' compensation program, in 1991. Since then, recovered memory claims have grown faster than any other kind of claim; moreover, the average recovered memory claim costs $9,127, compared with $1,997 for family sexual assault and $1,552 for a nonfamily sexual assault. See the series "Buried Memories, Broken Families," by Stephanie Salter and Carol Ness, in the San Francisco *Examiner*, April 4–9, 1993.

Childhood Abuse Is the First Step to Healing,'' said a 1992 ad from Adult Survivors of Child Abuse, a California treatment center, and that statement fairly characterizes the premise of the survivor movement. Along with an 800 number for counseling, the ad lists symptoms of repressed, as-yet-unrecovered memories of abuse: "mood swings, panic disorder, substance abuse, rage, flashbacks, depression, hopelessness, anxiety, paranoia, low self-esteem, relapse, relationship problems, sexual fear, sexual compulsion, self-mutilation, borderline personality, irritable bowel, migraine, P.M.S., post-traumatic stress, bulimia, anorexia, A.C.O.A. [adult child of an alcoholic], obesity, multiple personality, hallucinations, religious addiction, parenting problems, and suicidal feelings." This broad list parallels other checklists, in survivor books and workshops, where people are often told that the absence of memories of abuse is no indication that the abuse did not take place.

"Children often cope with abuse by forgetting it ever happened," write Bass and Davis in *The Courage to Heal*:

> As a result, you may have no conscious memory of being abused. You may have forgotten large chunks of your childhood. Yet there are things you do remember. When you are touched in a certain way, you feel nauseated. Certain words or facial expressions scare you. You know you never liked your mother to touch you. You slept with your clothes on in junior high school. You were taken to the doctor repeatedly for vaginal infections.
>
> You may think you don't have memories, but often as you begin to talk about what you do remember, there emerges a constellation of feelings, reactions, and recollections that add up to substantial information. To say "I was abused," you don't need the kind of recall that would stand up in a court of law.
>
> Often, the knowledge that you were abused starts with a tiny feeling, an intuition. It's important to trust that inner

voice and work from there. Assume your feelings are valid. So far, no one we've talked to thought she might have been abused, and then later discovered that she hadn't been. The progression always goes the other way, from suspicion to confirmation. If you think you were abused and your life shows the symptoms, then you were.

This argument is strikingly similar to the one advanced by Sigmund Freud in his paper "The Etiology of Hysteria," which he read to the Society for Psychiatry and Neurology in Vienna in the spring of 1896. At the beginning of his practice, Freud saw a number of patients, mostly women, who manifested the neurotic behavior of a then-popular diagnosis, hysteria. Bodily symptoms ranged from paralysis, tremors, hallucinations, blindness, deafness, chills, choking, vomiting, hiccuping, and a painful need to urinate, to name but a few. Linking this bewildering variety of symptoms was the fact that they were psychological in origin, although they masqueraded as physical disease. An example is a patient whose hand has gone numb. As a mental concept, the hand is a distinct entity, but from a neurological perspective it is a complex of nerves running from the fingers through the wrist and arm. There is not a single nerve that controls the hand, nor can the hand be divorced from other portions of the anatomy. Therefore the cause of the numbness must be psychological.

In this early paper, Freud postulated that hysteria was a reaction to traumatic events in childhood, which have been repressed: "Hysterical symptoms can be resolved if, starting from them, we are able to find the path back to the memory of a traumatic experience. If the memory which we have uncovered does not answer our expectations, it may be that we ought to pursue the same path a little further; perhaps behind the first traumatic scene there may be concealed the memory of a second, which satisfies our requirements better." What did he mean by that? Obviously Freud had an object in mind, a childhood event that was not only powerful enough to supply what he called the "traumatic force" that would give rise to hysterical symptoms in later life, but also sufficiently universal to account for the syndrome in each of his patients—the psychological virus, in other words, that would generate this neurotic disease.

Freud saw memory as a chain of associations; each symptom was attached to a particular chain, which would then call up another chain. For example, the symptom of hysterical vomiting may be associated with a memory of eating a rotten apple, and that memory itself may be linked to an earlier scene in which the patient discovered a putrid animal corpse while gathering windfalls in an orchard; that scene calls up another chain of memories, connected to another symptom, such as a headache. The task of the analyst is to retrace the pathways of memory through this converging chain of associations until arriving at what seems to be the traumatic source. Eventually, said Freud, "we come to the field of sexuality and to a small number of experiences which occur for the most part at the same period of life—namely, at puberty." At this point, however, there is a new disappointment for the analyst, because many of these experiences are "astonishingly trivial." He gave examples of one of his women patients whose neurosis seemed to be based on the experience of a boy who stroked her hand and, on a different occasion pressed his knee against her dress; for another patient, the traumatic event was an obscene riddle that had brought on an anxiety attack. Were they really such delicate flowers that they wilted under such tepid advances?

No, Freud reasoned; there must be yet another cause, further back in the chain of memories. "If we have the perseverance to press on with analysis into early childhood, as far back as a human memory is capable of reaching, we invariably bring the patient to reproduce experiences which, on account both of their peculiar features and of their relations to the symptoms of his later illness, must be regarded as the etiology of his neurosis for which we have been looking." To the dismay of his eminent colleagues in Vienna that day, Freud proposed that "at the bottom of every case of hysteria there are *one or more occurrences of premature sexual experience* [Freud's emphasis]."

Anticipating the objections that would arise from the suggestion that childhood sexual abuse was the "source of the Nile" in neuropathology, as he then believed, Freud defended himself by saying that doubts about the genuineness of these memories can be erased because of the anguish on the part of the patients as they remember scenes of seduction in childhood and their own resistance to believing in them once they have been produced. "While they are recalling these infantile experiences to consciousness, they suffer under the most violent sensations, of which they are ashamed and which they try to conceal; and, even after they have gone through them once more in such a convincing manner, they still attempt to withhold belief from them, by emphasizing the fact that, unlike what happens in the case of other forgotten material, they have no feeling of remembering the scenes." To Freud, the patients' distrust of their own memories was conclusive proof that they had not made them up. He was struck by the similarity in details that his patients reported. Either there was a conspiracy among the patients, or else they were suffering from nearly identical traumas. As for the obvious argument that the doctor himself had forced these memories onto his patients, through suggestion, that also seemed unlikely to Freud: "I have never yet succeeded in forcing on a patient a scene I was expecting to find."

There were, of course, many people who clearly recalled childhood sexual experiences who did not suffer from hysteria; as Freud pointed out, however, it was not the *memories* but the *repression* of them that caused hysterical behavior. The memories haven't disappeared; they've been shoved into the unconscious, where they work their poisonous influence until dragged into the light of awareness.

Freud spoke movingly of the reality of child abuse, which was rarely discussed in his time:

> All the singular conditions under which the ill-matched pair conduct their love-relations—on the one hand the adult, who cannot escape his share in the mutual dependence necessarily entailed by a sexual relationship, and yet is armed with complete authority and the right to punish, and can exchange the one role for the other to the uninhibited satisfaction of his moods, and on the other hand the child, who in his helplessness is at the mercy of this arbitrary will, who is prematurely aroused to every kind of sensibility and exposed to every sort of disappointment, and whose performance of the sexual activities assigned to him is often interrupted by his imperfect control of his natural needs—all these grotesque and yet tragic incongruities reveal themselves as stamped upon the later development of the individual and of his neurosis, in countless permanent effects which deserve to be traced in the greatest detail.

These passionate words were coldly received by Freud's colleagues, who believed that the stories of hysterics were lies or fantasies. To the formidable Richard von Krafft-Ebing, who was presiding over this conference, young Freud's remarks were "a scientific fairy tale." Moreover, there was the unstated implication that the abusers Freud was indicting in his daring seduction theory were respectable family men—such as the psychiatrists and neurologists gathered in Vienna that day. Indeed, Freud's theory was categorical. He had come to the conclusion privately that "in all cases, the *father*, not excluding my own, had to be accused of being perverse."

Freud suffered humiliating rejection and damage to his professional reputation. He would later be accused of rejecting his seduction theory out of a craven need to please his colleagues, who were almost exclusively male. There were other sources for his misgivings, however. In October of 1896, only a few months after Freud's disastrous presentation in Vienna, his own father died. During the grieving period that followed, Freud recognized that it was absurd to classify this lighthearted sage as a child molester, even though his own siblings showed traces of hysteria. His beloved theory was at war with his sense of reality. In order to account for the common diagnosis of hysteria, child abuse would have to be practically universal, since only a portion of the cases would give rise to neurotic illness. "Such widespread perversion against children is scarcely probable," he realized.

Adding to his qualms was the fact that some of his patients reported events that he took to be fantasies rather than memories. One of his patients reported that the devil himself had stuck pins in her fingers and placed a piece of candy on each drop of blood. "What would you say," Freud wrote to his friend Wilhelm Fliess, "if I told you that my brand-new theory of the early etiology of hysteria was already well known and had been published a hundred times over, though several centuries ago?" He was referring to the European witch trials. Freud was no believer in witches, and yet he wondered, "Why did the devil who took possession of the poor things invariably abuse them sexually and in a loathsome manner? Why are their confessions under torture so like the communications made by my patients in psychological treatment?" He had come to the same juncture that the profession he created would confront again a century later.

The abandonment of the seduction theory left Freud in a period of helplessness. In 1925, when he wrote his brief autobiography, a penitent but defensive tone is still apparent. "I must mention an error into which I fell for a while and which might well have had fatal consequences for the whole of my work," he wrote.

Under the pressure of the technical procedure* which I used at the time, the majority of my patients reproduced from their childhood scenes in which they were sexually seduced by some grown-up person. With female patients the part of seducer was almost always assigned to their father. I believed these stories, and consequently supposed that I had discovered the roots of the subsequent neurosis in these experiences of sexual seduction in childhood. My confidence was strengthened by a few cases in which relations of this kind with a father, uncle, or elder brother had continued up to an age at which memory was to be trusted. If the reader feels inclined to shake his head at my credulity, I cannot altogether blame him. . . . When, however, I was at last obliged to recognize that these scenes of seduction had never taken place, and that they were only fantasies which my patients had made up or which I myself had perhaps forced upon them, I was for some time completely at a loss. . . . When I had pulled myself together, I was able to draw the right conclusions from my discovery: namely, that the neurotic symptoms were not related directly to actual events but to fantasies embodying wishes, and that as far as the neurosis was concerned psychical reality was of more importance than material reality. I do not believe even now that I forced the seduction-fantasies upon my patients, that I "suggested" them. I had in fact stumbled for the first time upon the *Oedipus complex*, which was later to assume such an overwhelming importance, but which I did not recognize as yet in its disguise of fantasy. Moreover,

---

*Freud may have been referring to his early enthusiasm for hypnosis.

seduction during childhood retained a certain share, though a humbler one, in the etiology of neuroses. But the seducers turned out as a rule to have been older children. . . .

When the mistake had been cleared up, the path to the study of the sexual life of children lay open.

This momentous shift in Freud's perceptions was the turning point in his thinking and in the history of the psychoanalytic movement. It is important to note in his statement above that he never repudiated the reality of child abuse and its—admittedly, more modest—role in psychopathology. In his new understanding, Freud realized that his patients' fantasies were masking their own childhood sexual longings, and that what they were repressing were not actual seductions but their wishes for the same.

Freud compared the function of repression to that of a watchman who stands guard between the large entrance hall of the unconscious mind and the small drawing room in which consciousness resides. The watchman is a censor, examining mental impulses to determine whether they will be allowed to enter further. "If they have already pushed their way forward to the threshold and have been turned back by the watchman, then they are inadmissible to consciousness; we speak of them as *repressed*," Freud wrote. Such an impulse, for instance, might be the desire of a young girl for her father. The watchman would certainly frown on that; and although the image would be pushed back into the entrance hall, that doesn't mean that it is banished forever. Years, even decades, later, the forbidden desire might return, but this time in a clever and frightening disguise. In its exile from consciousness, the forbidden desire has become an unconscious fixation, enlarging itself on fantasies. "It ramifies like a fungus, so to speak, in the dark and takes on extreme forms of expression," Freud wrote in 1915, "which when translated and revealed to the neurotic are bound not merely to seem alien to him but to terrify him by the way in which they reflect an extraordinary and dangerous strength of instinct.'' In this way, Freud accounted for the bizarre nature of the fantasies his hysterical patients produced. The shameful sexual desire of a young girl for her father is reexperienced as her father's desire for her; her fantasy of sexual union is recast as a remembered assault.

An unfortunate consequence of Freud's rejection of his seduction theory was that society took a more skeptical stance toward all reports of child abuse, not merely those that had been achieved through recovered memories. That state of affairs began to change in the 1970s, as feminist writers began to speak up about the issues of rape and incest. The question of recovered memories did not arise; indeed, it was the persistence of memory, and not its repression, that was seen as the hallmark of childhood trauma.

Several forces produced the vector that we may call the recovered-memory phenomenon. Among them was the publication in 1980 of *Michelle Remembers*, which not only awakened popular interest in satanic-cult activity but also established the notion of massive repression, such that an entire secret life could be hidden away in the unconscious, waiting to be coaxed into consciousness by a caring, believing therapist. No longer ruled by psychiatry, the counseling profession itself was undergoing an informal deregulation. Psychologists and social workers were at least trained to practice, but increasingly counselors of varying ability and experience were simply being certified, or—as in Washington State—registered for a small fee, with no credentials required. Undersheriff Neil McClanahan, who has a bachelor's degree in human behavior from Evergreen State College, is a registered counselor; Pastor John Bratun is not registered, nor does he need to be unless he charges for his services. Bratun never even took a course in psychology in college; he was trained to be an art instructor, which is what he did before taking up counseling. The lack of credentials is not at all unusual. In New York, for instance, anyone can call himself a psychotherapist. This trend has left the profession prey to fads and malpractice.

At the same time, the field of psychotherapy was under attack within its own ranks. In 1984 two books appeared that challenged Freud's abandonment of the seduction theory: Alice Miller's *Thou Shalt Not Be Aware: Society's Betrayal of the Child* (which had been published in German three years earlier) and Jeffrey Moussaieff Masson's *The Assault on Truth: Freud's Suppression of the Seduction Theory*. These books struck a deep chord, coming at a time when child abuse suddenly seemed to be far more prevalent than society had ever been willing to recognize. A number of counselors began to wonder whether Freud had been right the first time; perhaps trauma—specifically, childhood sexual assault—really was at the root of most neurotic behavior, as Freud originally had claimed. (This revisionist theory quickly became so entrenched with some practitioners that they began calling themselves "traumatists" rather than therapists.) Using the same techniques that Freud himself renounced, particularly hypnosis, therapists and other counselors began uncovering memories of abuse which had apparently been repressed for most of the patient's life. In some cases, the patients reported abuse that had continued well into their teen or adult years, without being consciously acknowledged. Many of these patients were diagnosed as suffering from multiple-personality disorder.

Soon the discoveries in the counseling offices spilled out into the families and the communities, as patients were encouraged to confront their abusers, notify the police, or bring suit. "You cannot wait until you are doubt-free to disclose to your family," admonished Renee Fredrickson in her 1992 book, *Repressed Memories: A Journey of Recovery from Sexual Abuse*. "Avoid being tentative about your repressed memories. Do not just tell them; express them as truth. If months or years down the road, you find you are mistaken about details, you can always apologize and set the record straight."

Whether truthful or mistaken, recovered memories have had the effect of breaking apart thousands of families. A 1991 civil suit in Orange County, California, is characteristic of hundreds of cases that have flooded the legal system. Two adult daughters and a granddaughter accused their elderly mother/grandmother of gross, ritualistic crimes over a period of twenty-five years. The daughters contended that they had been tortured, sexually abused, and forced to kill babies in caves and church basements in Southern California. The women said that they had repressed the abuse until just a few years before, when the older daughter entered therapy after the breakup of her third marriage. In therapy she learned that she was a multiple personality, and she began remembering satanic-ritual abuse. Soon she brought her sister and her daughter (who was eleven when the trial began) into treatment with the same therapist, and they began having similar memories. Eventually all three were diagnosed as multiple personalities. They sought half a million dollars in damages. The defendant, who was a wealthy woman, contended that none of this abuse had ever happened. She believed that her older daughter was after her money, while her younger daughter and granddaughter were simply trying to please her older daughter. The jury decided that the defendant had neglected her daughters but had not intentionally harmed them. No damages were awarded. These claims have become sufficiently routine that some attorneys have standardized forms for their clients, in which the accusations of rape, torture, sodomy, and ritual abuse are already specified.

In 1992, in reaction to the rise of charges and lawsuits, a number of accused parents formed the False Memory Syndrome Foundation, in Philadelphia. By June of 1993, more than four thousand families had come forward (including the parents of Roseanne Arnold). The foundation discovered that these people had much in common. Most of their marriages—about 80 percent—were still intact, and usually only the husband had been accused, although wives had also been accused in nearly a third of the cases. The couples were also financially successful, with a median annual income of more than sixty thousand dollars. The majority had college educations. Most of them reported having frequently eaten meals together as a family and having gone on family vacations. More than half reported being active or very active in religion. About 17 percent of the accusations involved satanic-ritual abuse.

The accusers were adult children, 90 percent of them daughters. Most of the accusers had read *The Courage to Heal*. In 11 percent of the cases, siblings echoed the allegations, although 75 percent of the time the siblings did not believe the charges. Most strikingly, the accuser was a single child in only 2 percent of the families; larger families were predominant, with 3.62 children being the mean. Eleven percent of the families contained 5 children—the size of the Ingram household.

In almost every case, the allegations arose in therapy. It is difficult to know what part therapy may have played in the Ingram case. Julie was briefly in therapy before she made her outcry in her letter to her teacher. Ericka told the defense attorneys, "I'm going to a counselor and she's helping me to remember," but she would not elaborate or disclose the counselor's name. She also told Karla Franko, the speaker at the Heart to Heart camp, that she had gotten counseling, and she sought Franko's counseling over the phone.

Many people who feel themselves to be falsely accused believe that their children were coaxed or bullied into bringing charges by therapists or counselors who used their authority to persuade vulnerable clients that the complex problems they experience in adult life can be attributed to a single, simple cause: childhood abuse. Like their children, some of these aggrieved parents have taken their complaints to the courtroom by filing lawsuits against their children's therapists. There have also been cases brought by former clients who have recanted their stories of remembered abuse and charged their therapists with a form of mind control. Judges and juries all over the country are struggling with the concept of repression and the reality of recovered memories.

"In Salem, the conviction depended on how judges thought witches behaved," notes Paul McHugh, who is director of the Department of Psychiatry and Behavioral Sciences at Johns Hopkins University. "In our day, the conviction depends on how some therapists think a child's memory for trauma works." McHugh contends that "most severe traumas are not blocked out by children but are remembered all too well." He points to the memories of children from concentration camps and, more recently, to the children of Chowchilla, California, who were kidnapped in their school bus and buried in sand for many hours. They remembered their traumatic experience in excruciating, haunting detail. These children required psychiatric assistance "not to bring out forgotten material that was repressed, but to help them move away from a constant ruminative preoccupation with the experience," McHugh says.

McHugh finds a parallel between the recovered-memory phenomenon and an episode involving hysterics in nineteenth-century France. The distinguished neurologist and psychiatrist Jean-Martin Charcot was Freud's teacher at the Salpêtrière hospital in Paris. At one time, the hospital reorganized its patients and happened to place the hysterics in the same ward with epileptics. The hysterical patients began to display odd attacks that were similar to epileptic seizures, but different enough that Charcot believed he had discovered a new disorder, which he named "hystero-epilepsy." With his usual exactitude, he began to study this new condition. "Strangely, the patients became more and more disturbed, had more spells, and progressively more intriguing kinds of fits," McHugh relates. Audiences of doctors and the Parisian intelligentsia gathered to view this enthralling phenomenon. Finally, one of Charcot's students suggested that the great doctor had induced this behavior out of his own authority and enlarged it through his interest. Unless the doctor changed his approach to the patients, the student suggested, they would not improve.

As it developed, the student was correct. Two new methods of treatment were employed. First, the hysterics were isolated from the epileptics; and second, they were given a counter-suggestion, which offered the patients a different view than the one they currently held—that their condition was fascinating to Charcot. Instead of focusing on their condition, the staff began to turn to the question of the hysterics' life condition and the circumstances that had brought them into care into the first place. "This was the beginning of psychotherapy," writes McHugh in a paper titled "Historical Perspectives on Recovered Memories":

> How does this set of events relate to repressed memories? Charcot showed that just as there was epilepsy, it was also possible to create a pseudo-epilepsy. If one had a pseudo-epilepsy and focused on its counterfeit manifestations, they would worsen. If the patient remained amongst groups with both epilepsy and pseudo-epilepsy, she would not improve. The patient does improve when diagnostically distinguished from the actual epileptics and a common-sense management then devised.
>
> In the contemporary era patients who were sexually abused and those with pseudo-memories of sex abuse are often placed together by therapists in "incest survival" groups. The patients with the pseudo-memories tend to develop progressively more complicated and even quite implausible memories of their abusive childhood. Particular ideas seem quite

contagious and spread throughout the group—such as satanic-cult explanations for parental excesses and vile abuse including cannibalism. The patients often do not get better. Years of therapy continue to keep many of these repressed-memory patients angry, misinformed. The lesson from Paris is that it is crucial in practice to differentiate the incest-injured from those with false memories.

In 1987, Judith Lewis Herman and Emily Schatzow of the Women's Mental Health Collective in Somerville, Massachusetts, published a study of fifty-three female participants in a therapy group for incest survivors, such as McHugh describes. The paper was titled "Recovery and Verification of Memories of Childhood Sexual Trauma," and it is often cited by those who believe that abuse that has been remembered through recovered-memory therapy is just as real as abuse that has never been forgotten. The object of the study was to determine the link between traumatic childhood memories and symptoms in later life, and "to lay to rest, if possible, the concern that such recollections might be based on fantasy." Finally, the authors wished to explore the therapeutic effect of recovering and validating memories of early trauma.

All of the patients either reported having been sexually abused by a relative or else strongly suspected that was the case but could not remember. The sexual experiences the women described ranged from indecent exposure and propositions, which involved no actual physical contact, to vaginal or anal rape. Seventy-five percent named their fathers or step-fathers as the abusers. "In Freud's time, these women would undoubtedly have been diagnosed as suffering from hysteria," the authors stated. "They would readily have recognized their own afflictions in the anxiety attacks, the bodily disgust, the 'mental sensitiveness' and hyperactivity, the crying spells, the suicide attempts, and the 'outbursts of despair' that Freud described in his hysterical patients almost a century ago." In modern-day terminology, the women had received a variety of diagnoses, the most common being dysthymic disorder, which is a tendency to be despondent. Their backgrounds strongly resembled the family profiles described by the False Memory Syndrome Foundation survey.

Just over a quarter of the women reported severe memory deficits, which meant that they recalled little of their childhoods but were recovering or trying to recover memories of abuse. These patients stood out from the others. "Often they described almost complete amnesia for childhood experiences but reported recurrent images associated with extreme anxiety. Attempts at sexual intimacy often triggered flashback images of the abuser and panic states. These women were preoccupied with obsessive doubt over whether their victimization had been fantasized or real. Some had previously sought treatment with hypnosis or sodium amytal." When their memories erupted, they were often of a violent, sadistic, and grotesquely perverse character.

The authors claim that three-fourths of the women were able to obtain confirmation of their abuse from another source. They did not specify whether the fourth who were not able to do so was the same fourth with severe memory deficits—a significant omission, given their bold conclusion. The confirmations came from the perpetrator himself or other family members or from physical evidence, such as diaries or photographs. "The presumption that most patients' reports of childhood sexual abuse can be ascribed to fantasy no longer appears tenable," the authors asserted. "No positive evidence was adduced that would indicate that any of the patients' reports of sexual abuse were fantasized. In light of these findings, it would seem warranted to return to the insights offered by Freud's original statement on the etiology of hysteria, and to resume a line of investigation that the mental health professions prematurely abandoned 90 years ago. . . .

"Massive repression appeared to be the main defensive resource available to patients who were abused early in childhood and/or who suffered violent abuse.''*

Following up on the Herman-Schatzow study, John Briere, of the Department of Psychiatry at the University of Southern California School of Medicine, and Jon Conte, of the School of Social Work at the University of Washington, surveyed 420 females and 30 males who described themselves as having been sexually abused. They had been recruited by their therapists to respond to the study. "During the period of time between when the first forced sexual experience happened and your eighteenth birthday, was there ever a time when you could not remember the forced sexual experience?" the questioners asked. Nearly 60 percent responded yes. That figure is now being used as a benchmark for measuring the size of the population of people who were abused but repressed that memory, versus the number of those who were abused and never forgot.

---

*A more recent study, by Linda Meyer Williams at the Family Research Laboratory of the University of New Hampshire, located one hundred women who had reported abuse in 1973, 1974, or 1975 at a major northeastern hospital. The abuse ranged from fondling to intercourse, and the age of the females at the time they reported the abuse ranged from "infancy" to age twelve. In 1990 and 1991 the women were asked about childhood sexual experiences in order to elicit the memory of the reported abuse. Thirty-eight percent either forgot the abuse or chose not to report it. However, Williams does not say what percentage of them were infants when the offenses occurred. Those who were younger than four at the time could not be expected to remember much, if anything; nor is it likely that very young children would have been the primary reporters of abuse—presumably they had been taken to the hospital by a parent or caretaker who did the actual reporting.

However, there was no attempt to verify the abuse; the fact that the respondents remembered it was taken as sufficient evidence that it occurred. "It is likely that some significant proportion of psychotherapy clients who deny a history of childhood sexual victimization are, nevertheless, suffering from sexual abuse trauma," the authors concluded. They proposed that clinicians continue to entertain the hypothesis that their clients have been abused, even when there are no memories.

Briere and Conte also found, along with Herman and Schatzow, that the abuse recalled by those who claimed to have been amnesiac was far more violent than the abuse that had never been forgotten. But wouldn't more violent experiences also be more memorable? The theory that many have used to explain this paradox is that violence increases the level of repression; that subjects "dissociate" during the experience—that is, they mentally go away in order to protect themselves, then bury the pain in another part of their psyche, even in another personality. But if that is so, why don't children who experience other extreme forms of cruelty, such as life in a concentration camp, repress those memories or turn into multiple personalities? In one study, not a single child aged five to ten who had witnessed a parental murder had forgotten it. Why is it specifically sexual memories that are so often forgotten?

People often do forget details of traumatic events, especially when they are physically injured. Prosecutor Gary Tabor was in a traffic accident in college, but he can't remember a thing about it, except what people have told him. Sheriff Gary Edwards fell out of a tree he was pruning and lost the memory of the experience for ten years, until he was persuaded to take a bungee jump for a charitable event. Just before he jumped, the whole awful memory returned. In both cases, however, they knew something terrible had happened to them. Traumatic amnesia often accompanies combat or savage rapes, but the people who have suffered those experiences know what they've been through. It's the details that escape them.

Despite the common acceptance of the concept of repression, some clinical researchers, such as Loftus, make the point that repression has never been demonstrated experimentally. David S. Holmes of the University of Kansas has reviewed sixty years of attempts at proving the existence of repression. Early tests concentrated on subjects' ability to recall pleasant versus unpleasant memories. Unpleasant memories were less available, and this was taken as evidence of repression; but the same data also demonstrated that the more intense the memory, the more likely it was to be remembered, whether it was pleasant or unpleasant. Holmes himself conducted a study demonstrating that emotional intensity attached to unpleasant experiences declined over time at a greater rate than was the case with pleasant ones, thereby making unpleasant memories less memorable. Learning experiments were conducted in stressful versus nonstressful environments; when subjects were less able to remember the materials that they studied under stress, that, too, was taken as evidence of repression. However, those tests are better understood in terms of the difficulty of learning under stress. Other experiments presented insoluble problems to various personality types, with the hypothesis that certain individuals would be more likely to repress their failures. "The only consistent finding in this line of research was that subjects with a high need for achievement recalled more incompletions under high stress than low stress," Holmes reported. "They persisted in working on or thinking about their failures rather than repressing them. Not only do these findings fail to provide support for the concept of repression, but they are the opposite to what would be predicted on the basis of repression." Holmes concluded that it might be time to abandon the theory of repression. Of course, without the concept of repression, the edifice of psychoanalysis collapses.

Even if repression does function in the way that therapists who work with recovered memory suppose, is it possible to repress repeated, long-term abuses, some of which began in infancy and lasted well into adult years? This certainly goes far beyond what Freud had in mind. Richard Ofshe terms this new, aggrandized version "robust repression." The awkwardness of explaining this mechanism is evident in the answers that members of the Ingram family gave to investigators and defense attorneys. After Ingram had described a mass rape of his family by Rabie and Risch, Schoening asked, "They leave; then what—you as a family do what?"

"As I recall, I lock up the house and, uh, I don't recall any conversation," Ingram said. "It's kind of like, once the situation's over, we go into a different memory. . . . We're back to normal, if that's a way to put it."

Again, explaining how he would forget, as he drove home, that he had taken part in a satanic ritual, Ingram theorized, "At some point you block the memory and your conscious memory takes over. It's like I couldn't function up here on a day-to-day basis knowing what I had done."

Frequently, the victims remember being told not to remember. Sandy explained how she forgot having been raped on the kitchen floor by Rabie in August of 1988 this way: "Then he said . . . that I wouldn't remember anything and for me to finish washing the dishes." Ericka related that after a satanic ritual "my father would carry me back to my room and he would always say, 'You will not remember. You will not remember. This is a dream.' "

These theories were supported all along by the police officers and mental-health professionals who had been brought in to counsel the Ingrams and who often reassured the victims and the investigators alike that such wholesale, instant repression is completely normal.

"Tell me why it is that you wouldn't leave," Sax Rodgers

asked Sandy after she described newly recalled incidents of abuse.

"Well, what they've explained to me is that because of what happened to me, that I repressed everything as a defense or a survival mechanism, and that's why it's hard for me to remember. That it's all there and that I will remember it all, but it's . . ." She trailed off hopelessly. Her psychiatrist had provided her with this explanation.

One can see the handiwork of five different psychologists and counselors who talked to Ingram during six months of interrogations. "Two guys just anally rape you against your will, you say," Rodgers observed, referring to one of Ingram's accusations against Rabie and Risch. "You have been a police officer since 1972. . . . Why didn't you go report them?"

"I have also been a victim since I was five years old, and I learned very early that the easiest way to handle this was to hide it in unconscious memory, and then you don't have to deal with it," Ingram replied.

"The more severe the incident the deeper the repression and the more difficult it is to disclose," argues Undersheriff McClanahan. Like several of the other officers in this investigation, McClanahan sees himself as a psychological authority. He has written several papers on the Ingram case and has counseled with Olympia's survivor groups. Many members of these groups claim to have been ritually abused and have received diagnoses of multiple-personality disorder. McClanahan has also lectured on satanic-ritual abuse in survivor workshops. "Just to hear the words 'I believe you' can make all the difference in the world to a ritual-abuse survivor and oftentimes begins the process of trust, hope, and healing," McClanahan says. Those are words he has often spoken to Julie and Ericka Ingram.

These two hypotheses form the intellectual framework of the Ingram investigation: first, that the depth of the repression is a function of the intensity of the trauma; and, second, that victims must be believed. Once a victim's account is believed, however, the evidence must be stretched to fit it. Often, it's a big stretch. McClanahan accounts for the absence of scars on the Ingram daughters by saying that it is not uncommon for survivors to believe there are scars, because they've been conditioned to believe things that aren't true. He also explains why the sisters couldn't be given lie detector tests: "Our survivors are very traumatized. To question their credibility would cause them to be retraumatized. They're so fragile." In response to the fact that teams of officers and an anthropologist from the local college dug up the Ingram property looking for the burial ground of murdered babies and turned up only a single elk-bone fragment, McClanahan says that the ground was so acidic that the bones disintegrated. Months of the most extensive investigation in the county's history produced no physical evidence that any crimes or rituals ever took place, but Joe Vukich explains this by saying, "We shouldn't have found any. These guys were police officers. We expected to find a lot or nothing. We did find a couple pieces of bone. Obviously, something had happened."

In a paper that Elizabeth Loftus presented to the American Psychological Association in 1992, she asked, "Is it fair to compare the current growth of cases of repressed memory of child abuse to the witch crazes of several centuries ago?" Posing that question has caused her to become an object of scorn to many victims' advocates and to some other researchers who believe that her research is part of a social backlash against abused women and children. Loftus wrote about the "great fear" of witches that caused the witch-hunts to occur:

> There are some parallels but the differences are just as striking. In terms of similarities, some of the stories today are actually similar to stories of earlier times (e.g., witches flying

into bedrooms). In terms of differences, take a look at the accused and the accusers. In the most infamous witch-hunt in North America, 300 years ago in Salem, Massachusetts, three-fourths of the accused were women. Today, they are predominately (but not all) men. Witches in New England were mostly poor women over 40 who were misfits. . . . Today, the accused are often men of power and success. The witch accusations of past times were more often leveled by men, but today the accusations are predominately leveled by women. Today's phenomenon is more than anything a movement of the weak against the strong. There is today a "great fear" that grips our society, and that is fear of child abuse.

13

In February 1989, Jim Rabie and Ray Risch waived their right to a speedy trial in exchange for limited freedom: they were fitted with electronic bracelets and confined to their homes. It was just as well that they couldn't go out in public, for the satanic-ritual abuse allegations had surfaced in the pretrial hearings, and the county was in shock.

Richard Ofshe sent a report to the prosecutor outlining his concerns about the truthfulness of the alleged victims' stories. He pointed to the many inconsistencies in Ericka's accounts and her inability to recall anything about the ordinary life of the cult beyond the fact that "they chant." After his first interview with Ericka, she began to claim traumatic amnesia in order to explain the new information she was providing. No one had been able to confirm her stories. When Ofshe had asked Ericka why she hadn't moved out of her house sooner, if her life was so awful, she suggested that she didn't want to take a cut in her standard of living. "If she is capable of lying about numerous infant and adult murders and the other heinous acts of the group, one must seriously consider the possibility that all of her accusations are fabrications," Ofshe wrote. As for Julie, Ofshe believed that many of her accusations were false as well. "The timing with which she reveals information about the group is strangely similar to the timing with which her sister reveals information," he noted. "Even with her sister in the lead, Julie Ingram did little more than concur with her sister's report that a group existed." Ofshe discounted Paul's confessions because of the apparent ease with which he was persuaded to fantasize events and confess to imagined crimes, as he did in Ofshe's "little experiment." Sandy's statements were the result of a process of influence rather than real recollections based on memories of events, Ofshe wrote. "It is my opinion that Mrs. Ingram is not aware that she is inventing the scenes she came upon during the sessions with Reverend Bratun. I believe that she does not realize that the images are the result of her compliance to the demands of the situation. If she is permitted to continue to retell these stories over and over again her confidence in their validity will increase." Ofshe assured Tabor that there was no known technology available to Ingram, Rabie, and Risch that would induce Sandy's amnesia. "The implications of my opinions should be clear to anyone who reads this report," Ofshe concluded. "They are clear to me. I fear that my conscience would trouble me greatly were I not to communicate these conclusions to you in the most forceful and direct manner available. If I am correct in my judgment about the general truthfulness of Ericka and Julie Ingram and the extreme degree of suggestibility of Paul and Sandy Ingram there is a substantial danger that innocent people will be made to undergo a trial and a danger that they might be convicted."

When Tabor refused to turn the report over to the defense as exculpatory evidence—on the ground that, in his opinion, it was not real evidence—Ofshe complained to the presiding judge of the court. The judge agreed to make the report available to the defense attorneys. The report landed a shattering blow to the prosecution's already shaky case.

When Rabie and Risch were offered deals that would slash their jail time if they confessed, neither man would agree. In addition, other people who had been named by the daughters as members of the cult maintained their innocence, and there was no evidence to dispute their word. Beyond that, the months and months of work around the clock had taken an immense personal toll on the detectives. One marriage had ended. Tom Lynch had been a pal and fishing buddy of Sax Rodgers's, but their friendship broke apart over this case. Brian Schoening had begun dreaming about Ericka's abortion. He saw her lying on a table in a satanic ritual as her baby was being chopped up. At the end of the dream, the baby's little severed arm was forced into Ericka's vagina. Joe Vukich noticed that other officers were shying away from him in the hallway; he could only imagine how zombielike he must look to them. The fact that the investigation was consistently thwarted by a total lack of evidence added to the explosive pressures. The defense attorneys worried that Vukich, especially, was lurching out of control. During one court hearing, they stationed a private detective in a chair directly behind him because they were concerned that he might draw his gun and shoot the defendants.

What set this tinderbox ablaze was a discovery made thousands of miles away, in the Mexican border town of Matamoros, in April 1989. Police uncovered a ritual slaughterhouse on a ranch operated by a gang of drug smugglers. Thirteen mutilated corpses were exhumed, including that of twenty-one-year-old University of Texas student Mark Kilroy, who had been kidnapped as he walked across the international bridge toward Brownsville, Texas, a month before. The cult blended elements of witchcraft and Afro-Caribbean religions, but the main influence seems to have been a 1987 John Schlesinger film about devil worship called *The Believers*. The Matamoros cult lent an air of reality to the satanic hysteria that had taken root in the media. Agents for Geraldo Rivera and Oprah Winfrey were quickly on the scene.

"The discovery sent a shock wave through this part of Mexico and Texas and throughout the rest of the world," Rivera said on his show a couple of weeks later. "But, unbelievably bizarre as the Brownsville incident is, it is nothing viewers of this program haven't heard before." Rivera had on his show a former FBI agent named Ted Gunderson, who identified himself as a satanic-cult investigator. "I'd like to tell you right now, the next burial ground that we will learn about will be in Mason County, Washington," Gunderson announced, naming the county next door to Thurston County. "We've located a number of burial grounds in Mason County, and they can't possibly go out and dig them all up, because there's too many of them," he added.

Gunderson's announcement rocked the state of Washington. Soon he arrived and led a search team of private aircraft and television-news helicopters through the river valleys in the Olympic National Forest. Heat-seeking devices scanned the terrain, searching for the warmth of decomposing bodies. One of the helicopters landed on property belonging to Undersheriff McClanahan's parents. The searchers informed them that there was a satanic burial ground close by.

Although Thurston County authorities looked upon this frenzied hunt for bodies with official dismay, the truth is that they felt somewhat relieved, for the county had exhausted its own budget on the Ingram case and on the additional expense of conducting nighttime aircraft patrols that were intended to spot the bonfires of satanic cults. (Several fraternity beer busts had been raided.) Governor Booth Gardner now approved a $50,000 grant to continue the investigation, and the sheriff's office went to the state legislature seeking $750,000 for bullet-proof vests, night-viewing scopes, and electronic surveillance equipment. (That request was denied.) The sheriff's office also petitioned the county commissioners for $180,000. McClanahan showed the commissioners a short video about satanic-ritual abuse, in which a number of therapists spoke of the need for greater public support of its victims. "We are now hearing these reports from literally hundreds of therapists in every part of the United States that have amazing parallels," Dr. D. Corydon Hammond, a mild-faced professor at the University of Utah School of Medicine, said on the video. "What we are talking about here goes beyond child abuse or beyond the brainwashing of Patty Hearst or Korean War veterans. We're talking about people in some cases who . . . were raised in satanic cults from the time they were born—often cults that have come over from Europe, that have roots in the S.S. and death-camp squads, in some cases." The full extrapolation of Hammond's theory, not included on the video, goes on to postulate that the mind-control techniques used in such cults were developed by satanic Nazi scientists, who were captured by the CIA after the war and brought to the United States. The main figure was a Hasidic Jew, Dr. Green (an alias for Greenbaum), who saved himself from the gas chambers by assisting his Nazi captors and instructing them in the secrets of the cabala. Thus a note of anti-Semitism, which is almost always present in demonology, was sounded.* "The observa-

---

*According to Hammond, multiple personalities have been deliberately created in satanic ceremonies. "People say what's the purpose of it? My best guess is that the purpose of it is that they want an army of Manchurian Candidates, tens of thousands of mental robots who will do prostitution,

tions of experienced therapists leave little doubt that children in our society are at risk of being ritually abused," the narrator of the video concluded. "An appropriate response on the part of professionals requires that we be willing to suspend disbelief and begin to watch for the telltale indicators of this most severe and destructive form of child abuse." The commissioners granted the request, at a time when schoolteachers were unable to get a scheduled pay raise because of budget restrictions. Eventually, the Ingram investigation would cost three-quarters of a million dollars.

For weeks, Schoening and Vukich had pressured Ingram to come up with names of cult members to match the additional names that Julie had produced for Ofshe. Ingram had been praying and visualizing with Pastor Bratun, and when he was alone he fasted and spent much of his time speaking in tongues. On April 13, he began four days of disclosures, which produced ten names of past and present employees of the Thurston

do child pornography, smuggle drugs, engage in international arms smuggling, do snuff films—all sorts of very lucrative things—and do their bidding, and eventually, the megalomaniacs at the top believe, create a satanic order that will rule the world." The logic of SRA hysteria permits no other conclusion. Hammond, incidentally, was instrumental in persuading the governor of Utah to create a ritual-abuse task force. He reports that, largely as a result of this effort, 90 percent of the citizens of the state believe that SRA is real, and that there are two full-time ritual-abuse investigators working through the attorney general's office. According to the September 13, 1993, Salt Lake *Tribune*, the investigators spent $250,000 and found nothing to prosecute.

As for the mysterious Dr. Green, Sherrill A. Mulhern, an anthropologist at the University of Paris who has studied the SRA phenomenon, traces him to the 1989 Lisa Steinberg case in New York City. A Dr. Michael Green was supposedly a member of a cult that Joel Steinberg was in. See also Joyce Johnson, *What Lisa Knew: The Truths and Lies of the Steinberg Case* (G. P. Putnam's Sons, 1990).

County Sheriff's Office. He also named members of the canine unit—the actual dogs, not their handlers—and described a scene in which the animals raped Sandy.

That was too much, even for investigators who had been willing to believe everything so far. A parade of outraged employees of the sheriff's office took lie detector tests. All passed except one, and no one paid any attention to the man who failed. The common wisdom in the department now was that Paul Ingram had controlled the investigation from the beginning. This latest series of disclosures was his masterstroke, the thinking went; he had been protecting the cult all along, and by discrediting himself in this fashion he would ensure that his testimony was completely worthless. Even so, the demoralized detectives had to reconsider their case against Rabie and Risch. The possibility that the two were innocent apparently never arose in the discussion. The question was simply: Is there any way left to prosecute them—any evidence at all? As the case was falling apart, Ericka and Julie finally consented to allow Loreli Thompson to examine them for scars, the idea being that perhaps she could see something the doctor in Seattle could not. Thompson found nothing. Earlier, Ericka had told of being cut with a knife on her torso and had said she had a three-inch scar; but when she exposed her stomach and pointed to the area, Thompson couldn't see anything. Paula Davis thought she could see a slight line, but Thompson stretched the skin to make sure, and she still couldn't make it out. A family doctor finally said she had discovered a tiny, L-shaped scar, but no one else could discern it.

"I'm writing this to you to maybe help fill in the blank in your investigation," Julie stated in a letter to Tabor on April 26. She maintained that she really did have a scar on her left arm, from a time when her father had nailed her to the floor. She told of other scars from ceremonial incisions. Then she described a scene in which she had been tortured by her father,

Rabie, and Risch with a pair of pliers. Paul had visualized such a scene months before, and on several previous occasions Julie had denied that it had occurred. She also wrote: "One time, I was about 11, my mom open my private area w/them and put a piece of a died baby inside me. I did remove it after she left it was an arm." Apparently, Julie was now remembering Brian Schoening's dream.

"On May 1, 1989, the trials of Jim Rabie, Ray Risch and Paul Ingram are scheduled to begin," wrote McClanahan in an effort to buoy his depressed investigators. "This office has done a remarkable job in uncovering the first ritualistic abuse investigation that has been confirmed by an adult offender involved directly with the offenses in the nation's history. . . . Clearly we are on the cutting edge of knowledge being gained from ritual abuse." At the bottom of the letter, he appended the names of four therapists who were available to counsel the officers.

McClanahan had taken the trouble to put together a chart titled "The Formal Investigation of Ritual Abuse," which might be a model for similar investigations around the world. He was trained in "link analysis," and the chart attempted to place all the elements of the case into a display of associations. The centerpiece was a square, which McClanahan labeled "Ritual Abuse." Inside this box were four rectangles, titled "History," "Control," "Abuse," and "Organization," as well as two ovals, "Criminal" and "Non-Criminal." These were linked by tangents, forming a kind of web; and from each of these, other lines branched out to other rectangles and ovals outside the central square. From the "Abuse" rectangle, for instance, there were lines leading to "Physical," "Emotional," "Sexual," "Spiritual," and "Psychological" ovals. Each of those ovals, in turn, became a hub for new spokes radiating from it. From the "Psychological" oval, for instance, there were spokes labeled "Killing Babies," "Sacrifices," "Eating Urine/Feces," "Sex with Animals," "Self Pleasure," "Who Will Believe," "Tricked Humans/Animals Buried— Later Moved," "It's Victim's Fault Others Die," "Killing/ Eating Pets." A spoke from "Psychological" made a connection to yet another oval, "Concealment," which had its own sunburst of spokes, and each of them had subspokes: the "Victims Conditioning" spoke, for instance, branched into "Others Will Die If You Remember," "You Will Die If You Remember," and "Satan Can Read Your Mind." McClanahan was proud of his chart, which he hung prominently on his wall. It seemed to capture the multiplying complexity of the Ingram case and arrange it all into a single, comprehensible, if awe-inspiring, graphic display. The detectives, however, were mortified. "It looks like a schizophrenic's brain exploded on him," one of them remarked sourly.

Actually, the Ingram case was no longer a ritual-abuse investigation. All charges of satanic abuse had faded away as prosecutors worked to salvage something. Ingram spared them any further embarrassment by deciding to plead guilty to six counts of third-degree rape. On Bratun's advice, he had not read Ofshe's report, because it might confuse him. Both Ericka and Julie had written him, however, saying that he owed them a confession. Sandy, who had initiated divorce proceedings, also urged him to plead guilty. The judge delayed the sentencing when it was learned that Julie had been sent a threatening letter. "Hows my very special little girl?" the letter read. "Do you realize how much trouble you caused our family? You've really blow this one and to tell you the true you've broke us up forever you'll never be a part of our family again. You've hurt you mom so bad you've destroy her she wants to die . . . you do realize that there are many people that would like to see you dead and a few that are hunting for you." It was signed, "Your ex Father, Paul." As soon as Detective Thompson saw the letter, she recognized the handwriting: Julie had written it to herself. Undersheriff McClanahan explained the forgery as behavior typical of ritual-abuse victims, who have been conditioned to exaggerate. "She just wanted us to believe her," he said.

On May 3, 1989, two days after Ingram pleaded guilty, the prosecutor dropped the charges against Rabie and Risch. They had been in custody a hundred and fifty-eight days.

14

In May 1989, Richard Ofshe
had a telephone conversation with Paul Ingram in which he
urged him to try to withdraw his guilty plea before the sentencing. Ingram said that although he had been having doubts
himself about the validity of some of his memories, he was still
hopeful that he would be able to fill in the blanks with new
memories that would explain the many contradictions in his
own stories and those of his wife and children.

"I'll tell you something, Paul—you are never going to get
them," Ofshe said. "There is no way that you are going to be
able to remember anything that is going to reconcile all the
lies that have been told about this in the last few months."

"Assuming that you are right, you know I am still not
willing to make the girls get up on the stand if there is a chance
that I am going to emotionally damage them for the rest of
their lives," Ingram replied. He said both the prosecutor and
his own attorney had told them this might happen. Besides, he
still believed that he was repressing material that could explain
everything. "Let's even look at the guys that go through, like,
Vietnam," he added. "They hide a lot of those memories."

"Maybe somebody can blank out one event that was just
life-threatening to them, terrifying, disgusting beyond belief,"
Ofshe conceded. "Nobody can blank out as many events as

you think you blanked out—it has never happened," Ofshe went on. "Paul, everything that you have told me this evening adds up to one thing. There exists a process that you have learned to use that allows you to invent images that are consistent with what you think should be happening."

Ingram was unmoved.

Two months later, however, in his prison cell, he reconsidered. He had been keeping a log in which he divided his memories into three categories: "Definitely Happened," "Not So Definitely Happened," and "Not Sure." At the time of his plea, most of his memories had been lodged in the first category, but afterward they began an insidious migration into the other two. On the morning of July 19, 1989, the anxiety that had been building within him reached a crisis. While he was praying, he later related, he heard a murmur, "Let go of the rope." A deep feeling of peace settled over him. His mind began to clear. Suddenly, he could see that all the visualizations of rituals and abuse had been fantasies, not actual memories. He no longer believed that he was a satanist or a child abuser, or even the victim of child abuse himself. The experience approximated for him a religious conversion. He wrote in his Bible, "PRI DIED TO SELF 7-19-89."

Ingram got a new lawyer, who filed a motion to withdraw his guilty plea on the grounds that he had been coerced in the course of being interrogated and had given incriminating testimony while in a trancelike state. Unfortunately, it was too late to stop the train that Ingram boarded when he pleaded guilty. All the lawyer could do was to petition for leniency at the sentencing hearing, which took place in April of 1990.

"I'm Ericka Ingram. I was the daughter of Paul Ingram," Ericka stated in a surprise appearance at the hearing. Ericka wore a simple, pale dress, and she looked wan and stricken. She asked the judge to impose the greatest possible sentence.

Otherwise, "I believe he will either kill me or Julie," she warned. "He destroyed me and Julie's life and our entire family, and he doesn't care. He is obviously a very dangerous man." As she spoke, Schoening and Vukich sat in the back of the court and wept openly.

When Ericka finished, the judge asked Paul Ingram if he had anything to say.

Ingram rose and said in a clear voice, "I stand before you, I stand before God. I have never sexually abused my daughters. I am not guilty of these crimes." The judge showed no interest in this change of heart. Ordinarily, under the worst circumstances, Ingram would serve thirty-three to forty-three months for each count, running concurrently, which meant that he would be in prison for no more than three and a half years. The standards in the state of Washington are such that most first-time sex offenders receive a six-month sentence if they agree to urdergo treatment—a sentence Ingram had already served. The judge agreed with the prosecutor, however, that this was not an ordinary circumstance. Moreover, because Ingram was now saying that the events didn't happen, the judge believed that treatment would not be helpful. He sentenced Ingram to twenty years in prison, with the possibility of parole after twelve years.*

When the county prosecutor's office dropped the charges against Rabie and Risch, Ericka asked an attorney named Thomas Olmstead to file a suit against Thurston County for negligence in failing to supervise Ingram and Rabie.† Ericka

---

*Ingram's motion to withdraw his guilty plea was rejected by the appellate court in January of 1992, and by the Washington State Supreme Court in September of that same year. At this writing, the case is in federal court, but Ingram's chances there would appear to be slim, since the courts have shown little interest in granting an appeal to anyone who has pleaded guilty.
†The suit was still pending as this was written, in September 1993.

has asserted that some thirty satanists controlled the county and conspired to derail the case. Undersheriff McClanahan and Detective Schoening are among those Ericka has named as satanists. "How high does this go?" asks Olmstead, who is a fundamentalist Christian and a former FBI agent. "The governor? Who knows?"

Sandy Ingram, now divorced from Paul, has changed her name and lives in another town with Mark. Both Chad and Paul Ross have married and moved away. Ericka is living in California. Julie remains in the Olympia area, but she now uses a different name. The Ingram family, such as it was, has been destroyed. In the end, what had once held them together, their memories, is what blew them apart.

Jim Rabie and Ray Risch still live in Olympia, although they are widely believed to be guilty men who got away with heinous crimes. Risch works in the same automobile repair shop where he worked before, but he is rarely given any supervisory tasks. "There isn't a day that goes by that it doesn't get brought up," he says. "The cloud is still there. It's not a good memory." His wife reports that his mind is still scattered, and that it has been hard to keep up payments on their mobile home.

After abandoning his lobbying consultancy, Rabie worked for several months for a friend who owns a carpet shop, until customer complaints about his presence began to hurt business. Now he has a job with a vehicle-transport company. His legal bills, along with Risch's—which Rabie helped to pay— have exceeded ninety thousand dollars. Both men sued the county for false arrest and malicious prosecution, but their suit was dismissed by the United States District Court.* At this reporter's request, Rabie agreed to take another lie detector

---

*It was before the Ninth Circuit Court of Appeals at this writing.

test, which covered the same material as the one he had failed earlier. This time, he passed it.

As for the investigators, most of them have not altered their views. Undersheriff McClanahan, despite being denounced himself as a satanist by Ericka, remains unswayed. "Satanic abuse is real," he contends. "This case proves it."

Indeed, with Ingram's conviction, the case has become a primary exhibit in the SRA controversy. On December 2, 1991, many of the principals met in a television studio in New York. "Today, this woman will come face to face with the man that she says sexually tortured her in satanic rituals for seventeen years. A show you don't want to miss," said Sally Jessy Raphaël to her television audience. The camera focused on Ericka Ingram, wearing a cobalt-blue sweater and sitting meekly in a chair beside Raphaël. Arguably, it was shows like this one that created the Ingram fantasy in the first place.

"They were people in the community, like policemen," Ericka said as she described the cult. "There were some judges, doctors, lawyers. Different people in the community that had high political standings."

"What happened at the rituals?" Raphaël asked, her voice full of prodding compassion. "I know it must be pretty awful, but what happened?"

"First they would start with just, like, chanting," Ericka said. "Sometimes they would kill a baby."

"A baby?" Raphaël echoed. "Where would they get babies?"

"Sometimes people in the cult would have them just for this."

"Did this happen to you?" Raphaël asked. "You remember being on a table and people having sex with you?"

Ericka nodded.

"Wow. What else?"

"Sometimes they would drink blood," Ericka said. The members of the audience looked at her gravely and occasionally shook their heads in dismay. "One time, when I was sixteen, they gave me an abortion. I was five months pregnant. And the baby was still alive when they took it out. And they put it on top of me and then they cut it up. And then, when it was—when it was dead, then people in the group ate parts of it." A gasp arose from the thrilled audience. Later Ericka asserted, "I spent most of my life in the hospital. And that is true. And, I mean, doctors were just, like, looking at my body, just going—*ugh*!"

Raphaël introduced Jim Rabie, who was there trying to reclaim some of his reputation in the only forum available. "He says, even though he is innocent, his life, and that of his family, has been permanently damaged," Raphaël said.

"It destroyed a business that I had," Rabie explained, his voice cracking. "It has caused my family untold heartache."

But the audience wasn't interested in Rabie's problems. "Ericka, I feel so sorry for you," one woman in the audience said. "I have no idea why she would ever bring up this guy if he was not guilty."

Richard Ofshe was also on the show, matched against Bob Larson, a radio evangelist who has built his ministry by spreading satanic hysteria. "What is this whole thing about satanism, Dr. Ofshe?" Raphaël asked.

"Right now, there is an epidemic of these kinds of allegations in the country," Ofshe said. "They are totally unproven."

"There's an epidemic of satanism in the country, not allegations," Larson interjected.

"Why would you say there is this epidemic, as a sociologist?" Raphaël asked.

"In part because it's a way of reasserting the coherence and authority of fundamentalist perspectives in society," Ofshe said.

"All right, let's talk to Bob," said Raphaël, turning to the evangelist, who has thinning reddish-blond hair and a beard. "Bob, you've got a man here saying that in no case—and there have been one hundred court cases, I believe, maybe even more, involving satanic rituals in our country—in no case has there ever been any evidence, hard-core evidence, nor has anyone, except Ericka's father, ever said that they've done that. In other words, there's never been a confession."

"He's only technically correct," Larson said.

"Technically correct," Raphaël repeated flatly. When Larson cited the enormous number of people in therapy who have complained of satanic abuse, Raphaël asked again, "Why, if there are all these people under care, why isn't there one shred of evidence?"

"The difficulty is that the evidentiary basis of the justice system is not commensurate with what you deal with in a therapeutic process," Larson said. "When are we going to start believing people who come forward like this, instead of putting them through some type of legal litmus test?" One supposes that the "legal litmus test" he was referring to was the need for Ericka to provide credible testimony in order to convict Rabie of the crimes she accuses him of. Larson's voice rose in indignation. "These are people who suffered the most incredible abuse!" he cried. "My God! This woman has been defecated on, urinated on—"

"By him!" Ericka cried, pointing at the hapless Rabie.

"She's experienced bestiality and group sex by this man!" Larson said as he laid a pastoral hand on Ericka's knee. "When are we going to start believing the victims?"

"Believe us!" Ericka cried.

Epilogue

Four and a half years after his arrest, Paul Ingram, grayer now than he was during his legal hearings, lives in a prison in a state far from Washington. He is in protective custody, presumably for his own safety as a former police officer, but he has made no secret of his identity. Most of his fellow inmates know him as an editor of the prison newspaper. He also works as a clerk in the prison law library. He has always been drawn to the simple, regimented life, and prison is peculiarly agreeable to him. In certain respects, it resembles the cloistered life he might have chosen if he had followed his mother's wishes and become a priest. He says that he has found a deeper peace now than at any other point in his life.

"To be real honest, I have more questions about this than I have answers," he says of what happened to his family. His theory about why he "remembered" sexual and satanic abuse is that it helped him explain to himself why a man who was ostensibly a good Christian and a loving parent could have mistreated his children. "I wasn't a good father, I know," he admits. "I wasn't there for the kids. I wasn't able to communicate with them as I should have. I never sexually abused anybody. But emotional abuse—you don't like to admit it, but somebody has to. A child is a pretty delicate creature. I did a lot of hollering as a father, and I think that must have intimidated the kids. One time, Julie ran a bath that was too hot and she scalded Mark. I slapped her. Another time, she tried to run away. I saw her running down the driveway and Sandy chasing her. She was about sixteen. I ran out and caught her and pulled her hair and said she was coming back home. I remember hitting Paul Ross once on the back of the head, and I kicked him. But I never beat my children. When I got angry, that's when I hollered. There was a lack of affection they should get from a father figure."

Is that all? Certainly that would be the most frightening conclusion of the Ingram case, that the bonds of family life are so intricately framed that such appalling perversions of memory can arise from ordinary rotten behavior.

Were there real acts of sexual abuse in the Ingram household? The testimony of the family members about this is as contradictory as it is for the ritual abuse. Despite the months of intense, unrelenting interrogation of Paul Ingram, and dozens of conflicting episodes remembered by Ingram and his wife and children, the six counts of third-degree rape that Ingram was charged with were all based on confessions elicited in the two days immediately after his arrest; they emerged in sessions with Schoening and Vukich—and, in part, with psychologist Richard Peterson and Pastor John Bratun—during which, Ingram says, he was repeatedly assured that he would remember the abuse once he had confessed to it. Here, for instance, is the text of his confession to one of the rapes he was eventually charged with:

Q: Let's try to talk about the most recent time, Paul. Ericka tells me that it was toward the end of September, just before she moved out. Do you remember that?

A: Well, I keep trying to, to recollect it, and I'm still kind of looking at it as a third party, but, uh, the evidence,

and I am trying to put this in the first person, it's not comin'
very well, but, uh, I would've gotten out of bed, put on a
bathrobe, gone into her room, taken the robe off and at least
partially disrobing her and then fondling, uh, her breasts and
her vagina and, uh, also telling her that if she ever told anybody that, that I would, uh, kill her. . . .

Q: Now you've talked about this in the third party. I'm
going to ask you directly, is this what happened?

A: Whew, I'm still having trouble gettin' a clear picture
of what happened. I—I know in my own mind that these
things had to have happened.

The fact that all the memories of the family members became less believable over time caused the prosecution to return
to these early statements as the "core truth" of the Ingram
case. The fundamental premise of the investigation was that
something must have happened. At no time did the detectives
ever consider the possibility that the source of the memories
was the investigation itself—there was no other reality. In
the end, all that was salvageable was Ingram's experimental
attempt to find the memories in his mind by confessing to
them.

There was another possibility that the detectives did not
pursue. From the beginning, both of the Ingram daughters
had said that they had sex with their brothers. Julie wrote in
one of her statements to Loreli Thompson that when she was
thirteen Paul Ross had taken her into his room and they had
intercourse on his bed. In Joe Vukich's sole interview with
Paula Davis, Davis recalled Ericka's first disclosure to her, in
the summer of 1988, before the Heart to Heart camp. Ericka
had been sitting for Davis's children, and when Davis got
home she had sat down with Ericka on the couch, "and she
told me."

Q. What did she tell you?

A. First she told me about her brother. She told me that Chad had had sex—her brothers both, but mostly she was talking about Chad—that her brothers had had sex with her for a lot of years since she was little.

Q. That's Chad and Paul Jr.?

A. Yes . . .

Q. Did she say anything about her father on this particular occasion?

A. No, she did not. In fact, I asked her, and she looked at me really strange and shook her head no.

The detectives chose to believe that even if there was sexual acting out among the siblings, such behavior must have been learned—presumably through abuse by the parents.

All of these scenarios of abuse are confounded by the Ingram daughters' frequent claims that they were actually virgins. The medical evidence placed into the records does not specify whether they were or were not. If it was true that Ericka was a virgin, then Karla Franko's pronouncement at the church camp (that God had revealed to her that Ericka had been sexually abused) would answer what may have been an irreconcilable dilemma for her. In 1987, Ericka had driven to California with her friend Paula Davis. On the way Ericka became so ill that she had to check into a hospital. The examining doctor said she was suffering from pelvic inflammatory disease. When Davis asked the doctor how Ericka might have contracted such an infection, he told her that it is spread through sexual intercourse. Later, when Ericka was trying to bolster her case with the detectives, she pointed to the infection as proof of her abuse. The doctor had failed to mention, however, that pelvic inflammatory disease can also be caused by an ovarian cyst, which in fact Ericka did have, although it had not been diagnosed on that visit.

The sexual content of the memories that Paul Ingram and his daughters produced was on its face a tragic courtship of buried longings forced into public view. Neither daughter ever visualized the other in these fantasies, although in real life they were almost constantly together. One can read them as competitive bids for their father's favor. Each memory began by seeing him enter their room and choose now Julie, now Ericka, at the expense of the other. The unchosen daughter is either mysteriously absent or so deeply asleep as to be completely unconscious. One can appreciate in these richly envisioned fantasies the sexual power that underlies the dynamics of the family, and the anger that accumulates and gradually replaces the unrequited love of a needy child for an unavailable parent. Seen in this manner, the Ingram case becomes a vivid illustration of exactly why Freud abandoned the seduction theory in favor of the Oedipus complex. If the memories of the Ingram family are not real events, then perhaps they arise from repressed wishes.

Ritual abuse cases have much in common; indeed, this is often taken as proof of the existence of a single, all-powerful satanic network. It can also be interpreted as evidence of the common fantasy life that has been a feature of our culture for centuries. The myth of ritual murder arose in Europe in the twelfth century, and by the fifteenth century the blood libel attached to the Jews had reached a frenzy. It began to die out only as the Reformation approached. By then, of course, the Inquisition had turned its implacable eye on witches. One of the fascinating details of the European witch-hunts, which didn't end until 1700, is that frequently the witches' confessions—like Paul Ingram's—were voluntary and apparently deeply believed in. The elements of sodomy, incest, pedophilia, cannibalism, and the ritual use of human blood appear to be universal elements of demonology in all cultures.* They correspond to inherent human fears and taboos.

As for why the satanic-ritual hysteria would appear again in our century, one can point to the rise of fundamentalist religions, the social anxiety about the loss of traditional values, and political uncertainty following the collapse of international communism. In addition, one can't help noticing the repeated theme of abortion. Both Ericka and Julie talked about receiving abortions and having their babies cut up and rubbed on them. This seems to be an element of nearly every SRA account. The imagery of babies being cut up and sacrificed is also a prominent feature of antiabortion protest. It is only a theory, but perhaps the psychic damage done by the abortion debate is reflected in the anguished fantasies of so many young women.

Religion certainly played a guiding role in the Ingram case. Every member of the Ingram family was primed to believe in the existence of satanic cults. Still, their belief had as much to do with popular culture and tabloid television as it did with their church. The doctrine of the Church of Living Water is that Satan is real and walks the earth, which is similar to the beliefs of many more widely recognized Protestant denominations. The rigid nature of the Ingrams' personal beliefs may have made them particularly susceptible to the notion that the family had lived two opposing lives—one as prominent Chris-

---

*Cf. Phillips Stevens, Jr., "Universal Cultural Elements in the Satanic Demonology," *Journal of Psychology and Theology* 20, no. 3 (Fall 1992). There are other common elements of folklore involved in the Ingram case—notably, Chad Ingram's dream of the witch that comes into his window and sits on his chest. This common nightmare is known as an "Old Hag attack" in Newfoundland, where it has been extensively studied. David J. Hufford has written about this fascinating phenomenon, in both Newfoundland and the United States, in *The Terror That Comes in the Night: An Experience-Centered Study of Supernatural Assault Traditions* (University of Pennsylvania Press, 1982).

tians in their church and their community, the other as covert practicing satanists—and also that the good and aboveboard public life of the family was entirely unaware of its furtive, monstrous underlife. One must also acknowledge that the religious beliefs of some of the investigators may have figured into their pursuing the case well past the point of logical inconsistency. The bending of all evidence to support the absurdity of an insupportable proposition is the very nature of a witch-hunt.

On the other hand, not all of the investigators were deeply religious people. Their judgment may have been clouded by more common assumptions about the nature of human memory. Memory is not like videotape, as Jim Rabie's polygraph examiner believes. What we have learned about this miraculous and mysterious capacity is that it is reconstructive, that it continually recreates itself, continually reinvents personal history. Freud anticipated much of modern-day research on this subject when he wrote, in 1899:

> It may indeed be questioned whether we have any memories at all *from* our childhood: memories *relating* to our childhood may be all we possess. Our childhood memories show us our earliest years not as they were but as they appeared at the later periods when the memories were aroused. In these periods of arousal, the childhood memories did not, as people are accustomed to say, *emerge*; they were *formed* at that time. And a number of motives with no concern for historical accuracy, had a part in forming them, as well as in the selection of the memories themselves.

Whatever the true nature of human memory, the Ingram case makes obvious the perils of a fixed idea—in this instance, the fixed idea being that the truth of human behavior, and even of one's own experience, can be cloaked by a trick of the unconscious mind, which draws a curtain of amnesia over a painful past. Unfortunately, the theory of repression, in its current "robust" form, also permits the construction of imaginary alternative lives, which may contain some symbolic truth but are in other respects damaging counterfeits that corrupt the currency of real experience.

One could say that the miracle of the Ingram case is that it did not go further than it did. If Ingram's memories had not finally become too absurd even for the investigators to believe, if Rabie or Risch had accepted the prosecutor's deals, if the alleged crimes of other people implicated in the investigation had occurred within the statute of limitations—if any of these quite conceivable scenarios had taken place, then the witch-hunt in Olympia would have raged out of control, and one cannot guess how many other lives might have been destroyed. But, unfortunately, what happened to the Ingram family, and to Ray Risch and Jim Rabie, is actually happening to thousands of other people throughout the country who have been accused on the basis of recovered memories. Perhaps some of these memories are real; certainly many are false. Whatever the value of repression as a scientific concept or a therapeutic tool, unquestioning belief in it has become as dangerous as the belief in witches. One idea is modern and the other an artifact of what we like to think of as a credulous age, but the consequences are depressingly the same.

A Note on Sources and
a Few Words About Journalism

The investigative files into the case of Paul Ingram and those of Jim Rabie and Ray Risch occupy many boxes in the Thurston County Courthouse, and they were the primary material for much of this book. Some of these interview sessions were recorded, although only a few such tapes survive. Those that do provide a better understanding of the emotional interactions between the investigators and the victims and the suspects who were caught up in this extraordinary affair.

Most of the investigators spoke freely to me (I was not able to talk to Tom Lynch or Paul Johnson). All of the detectives I dealt with were helpful and candid. I also interviewed various people in the prosecutor's office, including Patrick Sutherland, David Klumpp, and in particular Gary Tabor, who gave generously of his time and made many materials available to me. Psychologist Richard Peterson agreed to speak to me on two occasions. In addition, I interviewed Jim Rabie and Ray Risch; their wives, Ruth and Jodie; defense attorneys G. Saxon Rodgers, Judith Weigand, Wayne Fricke, and Gary Preble; many members of the Church of Living Water (although not Pastor John Bratun, who no longer serves as associate pastor); friends of the Ingram family and teachers of the Ingram children; Kenneth Lanning of the FBI; Karla Franko; Tyra Lindquist and Ann Bridges at Safeplace; Bart Potter, the former *Olympian* reporter who covered the case; Mark Papworth, an anthropologist at Evergreen State College, who supervised the excavation and search of the Ingram property; Richard Ofshe; psychologist Chris Hatcher, director of the Center for the Study of Trauma at the University of California, who spoke with members of the Ingram family on behalf of the prosecution; and psychiatrist Dr. Alan Traywick, counselor Geri Walter, and therapists Margaret Cain Roberts and Sydney Gienty, all of whom gave me the benefit of their perspectives without compromising their relationships with their clients.

When I attribute thoughts or reactions to people in this book, they themselves are the sources, through either personal interviews or statements they have made on the record. Frequently a scene will have several sources with conflicting perspectives; for instance, the scene in which Richard Ofshe performs his "little experiment." Not only Ofshe but also Brian Schoening, Joe Vukich, and Paul Ingram participated in that discussion and shared with me their versions of the event. Where I have quoted dialogue in that scene, it consists of the words each man attributed to himself.

I was able to interview Paul Ingram several times, by phone and letter and in person; Julie I interviewed once, in the presence of Loreli Thompson, for a period of three hours; Chad spoke to me over the phone on several occasions. Sandy and Ericka chose not to be interviewed, and Paul Ross could not be found. Paul's sister Robin Ingram was also quite helpful in providing family background. Where I have quoted family members I did not talk to, or attributed reactions to them (such as Sandy's surprise when the detectives told her that her husband was a homosexual), such material comes from their interviews with the investigators or statements in court hearings or in the valuable recorded interviews with Ofshe. Sandy and Paul both kept diaries (Sandy's is actually a series of notes to herself on scratch paper which form a haphazard log), which were made part of the record. In addition, Paul has written several accounts of his life, in letters to friends and in a lengthy letter to journalist Ethan Watters, which were available to me.

There have been several other accounts of the Ingram case. Richard Ofshe wrote about it in a paper titled "Inadvertent Hypnosis during Interrogation: False Confession Due to Dissociative State; Mis-Identified Multiple Personality and the Satanic Cult Hypothesis," which was published as the lead article in the *International Journal of Clinical and Experimental Hypnosis* 40, no. 3 (1992). In addition, there was the seminal article by Ethan Watters in the July/August 1991 *Mother Jones*, titled "The Devil in Mr. Ingram." The only critical account in Olympia was an excellent series by Chris Bader, a student at Evergreen State College, which appeared from October to December 1991 in the *Cooper Point Journal*, the student newspaper. I have had the benefit of their insights and research.

In some cases, lengthy interviews have been compressed to be made more succinct, although, I believe, with no loss of context. If material is excerpted within a statement, the abridgment is indicated by an ellipsis. It is a convention of journalism, which I subscribe to, that when a quote closes, the next quote may actually skip over the dross that so often fills the spaces of open conversation. For instance, when the polygraph operator asks Jim Rabie, "Have you ever found yourself to be vindictive?" I have Rabie respond simply, "When provoked, and my anger is really high, I can be vindictive, yes." The actual response is:

> A bit within—uh—one thing I—I try never to say something that I can't back up. I try never to say anything that isn't true and so if I—even in anger—say something, I may be very vindictive in saying too much of the truth. I don't, uh, make up something or say something that isn't the truth. Yet, I—I hurt Ruth once in a while because she's got some

very sensitive areas, and I know that, and if we get into an argument that I may bring it up or say something about some things that are very painful to her. So in some respects, I am probably a little bit vindictive and it—it's not, not that much. I mean, it isn't a constant thing, by any means. But when provoked, when my anger is really high, I can be vindictive, yes.

This is not at all an extravagant or unusual example, because this is what real conversation often looks like, when exactly transcribed. It is the same with a reporter's notes or tapes of an interview. The reporter has a duty to sort through such material and draw out the pertinent statements. It is the reporter's job, and his badge of honor, to present this material fairly and let the reader draw his own conclusions. But it is the writer's job to prune away needless, ungainly verbiage and make the reader's experience as interesting and pleasurable as possible. The reader should not have to recapitulate the boredom and frustration and confusion that the reporter endured while uncovering the story and that the writer suffered while trying to make it comprehensible. I feel the need to make such statements only because of the lowered level of public trust where journalists are concerned.

I arranged and paid for Jim Rabie's second lie detector test from an independent polygraph operator in another county. As a reporter, I do not use polygraphs, nor do I believe that they should be used in court, because of their questionable accuracy. The decision to use the polygraph in this case was a writer's decision. I supposed that for some readers Rabie's failure to pass the lie detector test would be nearly conclusive proof of his guilt. In my mind, it was not; however, it seemed obligatory to test him again in order to represent the interest of the readers who believe strongly in the efficacy of such devices.

On the subjects of memory, hypnosis, and the subtleties of psychological states, I drew upon the books and papers cited in the text, as well as personal interviews with Dr. George K. Ganaway, Dr. Paul McHugh, Ricardo Ainslie, Jev and Sydnor Sikes, Elizabeth Loftus, Dr. Harold I. Lief, Dr. Judith Lewis Herman, Margaret Singer, Randy Noblitt, Hollida Wakefield, Michael Nash, Linda Meyer Williams, Fred Frankel, Stuart Grassion, and Martha Rogers. I also relied on *Repression and Dissociation: Implications for Personality Theory, Psychopathology, and Health*, Jerome L. Singer, editor (University of Chicago Press, 1990); *Hidden Memories*, by Robert A. Baker (Prometheus Books, 1992); and *Trauma and Recovery*, by Judith Lewis Herman (Basic Books, 1992); and the Standard Edition works (translated and edited by James Strachey) of Freud. In addition, I want to thank Urs Frei and Susan Engel for their thoughtful letters on the subject of repression. On the folklore of satanic-ritual abuse, I was able to talk with Sherrill Mulhern at the University of Paris, Jeffrey S. Victor of SUNY, and journalist Debbie Nathan, who has done ground-breaking work in this field. I also referred to Victor's *Satanic Panic: The Creation of a Contemporary Legend* (Open Court, 1993); *The Satanism Scare*, James T. Richardson, Joel Best, and David G. Bromley, editors (Aldine de Gruyter, 1991); *The Myth of Ritual Murder: Jews and Magic in Reformation Germany*, by R. Po-chia Hsia; and *The Witches' Advocate: Basque Witchcraft and the Spanish Inquisition*, by Gustav Henningsen (University of Nevada Press, 1980).

As is evident, this book is a collaboration of the thought and goodwill of many people, and I thank them for their kindness.